Testing for Language Teachers

CAMBRIDGE HANDBOOKS FOR LANGUAGE TEACHERS
General Editors: Michael Swan and Roger Bowers

This is a series of practical guides for teachers of English and other
languages. Illustrative examples are usually drawn from the field of English
as a foreign or second language, but the ideas and techniques described can
equally well be used in the teaching of any language.

In this series:

Drama Techniques in Language Learning – A resource book of
communication activities for language teachers
by Alan Maley and Alan Duff

Games for Language Learning
by Andrew Wright, David Betteridge and Michael Buckby

Discussions that Work – Task-centred fluency practice *by Penny Ur*

Once Upon a Time – Using stories in the language classroom
by John Morgan and Mario Rinvolucri

Teaching Listening Comprehension *by Penny Ur*

Keep Talking – Communicative fluency activities for language teaching
by Frederike Klippel

Working with Words – A guide to teaching and learning vocabulary
by Ruth Gairns and Stuart Redman

Learner English – A teacher's guide to interference and other problems
edited by Michael Swan and Bernard Smith

Testing Spoken Language – A handbook of oral testing techniques
by Nic Underhill

Literature in the Language Classroom – A resource book of ideas and
activities *by Joanne Collie and Stephen Slater*

Dictation – New methods, new possibilities
by Paul Davis and Mario Rinvolucri

Grammar Practice Activities – A practical guide for teachers *by Penny Ur*

Testing for Language Teachers *by Arthur Hughes*

Testing for Language Teachers

Arthur Hughes

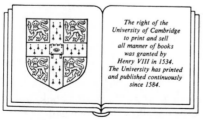

The right of the
University of Cambridge
to print and sell
all manner of books
was granted by
Henry VIII in 1534.
The University has printed
and published continuously
since 1584.

Cambridge University Press
Cambridge
New York   Port Chester
Melbourne   Sydney

Published by the Press Syndicate of the University of Cambridge
The Pitt Building, Trumpington Street, Cambridge CB2 1RP
40 West 20th Street, New York, NY 10011, USA
10 Stamford Road, Oakleigh, Melbourne 3166, Australia

© Cambridge University Press 1989

First published 1989

Printed in Great Britain
by Bell & Bain Ltd, Glasgow

Library of Congress cataloguing in publication data

Hughes, Arthur, 1941–
Testing for language teachers / Arthur Hughes.
     p.   cm. – (Cambridge handbooks for language teachers)
Bibliography: p.
Includes index.
ISBN 0 521 25264 4. – ISBN 0 521 27260 2 (pbk.)
1. Language and languages – Ability testing.   I. Title.
II. Series.
P53.4.H84   1989
407.6–dc19   88–3850 CIP

British Library cataloguing in publication data

Hughes, Arthur, 1941–
Testing for language teachers. – (Cambridge
handbooks for language teachers).
1. Great Britain. Educational institutions.
Students. Foreign language skills.
Assessment. Tests – For teaching.
I. Title.
418'.0076

ISBN 0 521 25264 4 hard covers
ISBN 0 521 27260 2 paperback

CE

For Vicky, Meg and Jake

Contents

Acknowledgements

The author and publishers would like to thank the following for permission to reproduce copyright material:

American Council on the Teaching of Foreign Languages Inc. for extracts from ACTFL Provisional Proficiency Guidelines and Generic Guidelines (1986); ARELS Examination Trust for extracts from examinations; A. Hughes for extracts from the New Boğaziçi University Language Proficiency Test (1984); The British Council for the draft of the scale for ELTS test; Cambridge University Press for M. Swan and C. Walter: *Cambridge English Course* 3, p. 16 (1988); Educational Testing Services for the graph on p. 84; Filmscan Lingual House for M. Garman and A. Hughes: *English Cloze Exercises* Chapter 4 (1983); The Foreign Service Institute for the *Testing Kit* pp. 35–8 (1979); Harper & Row, Publishers, Inc. for the graph on p. 161, from *Basic Statistical Methods* by N. M. Downie and Robert W. Heath, copyright © 1985 in N. M. Downie and Robert W. Heath, reprinted with permission of Harper & Row, Publishers, Inc.; *The Independent* for N. Timmins: 'Passive smoking comes under fire', 14 March 1987; Joint Matriculation Board for extracts from March 1980 and June 1980 Tests in English (Overseas); *Language Learning*, and J. W. Oller Jr. and C. A. Conrad for the extract from 'The cloze technique and ESL proficiency', *Language Learning* 21:183–94; Longman UK Ltd for D. Byrne: *Progressive Picture Compositions* p. 30 (1967); Macmillan London Ltd for Colin Dexter: *The Secret of Annexe 3* (1986); *The Observer* for S. Limb: 'One-sided headache', 9 October 1983; The Royal Society of Arts Examinations Board/University of Cambridge Local Examinations Syndicate for extracts from the specifications for the examination in *The Communicative Use of English as a Foreign Language*, and from the 1984 and 1985 summer examinations; The University of Cambridge Local Examinations Syndicate for the extract from *Testpack 1* paper 3; The University of Oxford Delegacy of Local Examinations for extracts from the Oxford Examination in English as a Foreign Languge.

Preface

The simple objective of this book is to help language teachers write better tests. It takes the view that test construction is essentially a matter of problem solving, with every teaching situation setting a different testing problem. In order to arrive at the best solution for any particular situation – the most appropriate test or testing system – it is not enough to have at one's disposal a collection of test techniques from which to choose. It is also necessary to understand the principles of testing and how they can be applied in practice.

It is relatively straightforward to introduce and explain the desirable qualities of tests: validity, reliability, practicality, and beneficial backwash (this last, which refers to the favourable effects tests can have on teaching and learning, here receiving more attention than is usual in books of this kind). It is much less easy to give realistic advice on how to achieve them in teacher-made tests. One is tempted either to ignore the problem or to present as a model the not always appropriate methods of large-scale testing institutions. In resisting these temptations I have been compelled to make explicit in my own mind much that had previously been vague and intuitive. I have certainly benefited from doing this; I hope that readers will too.

Exemplification throughout the book is from the testing of English as a foreign language. This reflects both my own experience in language testing and the fact that English will be the one language known by all readers. I trust that it will not prove too difficult for teachers of other languages to find or construct parallel examples of their own.

I must acknowledge the contributions of others: MA students at Reading University, too numerous to mention by name, who have taught me much, usually by asking questions that I could not answer; my friends and colleagues, Paul Fletcher, Michael Garman, Don Porter, and Tony Woods, who all read parts of the manuscript and made many helpful suggestions; Barbara Barnes, who typed a first version of the early chapters; Michael Swan, who gave good advice and much encouragement, and who remained remarkably patient as each deadline for completion passed; and finally my family, who accepted the writing of the book as an excuse more often than they should. To all of them I am very grateful.

1 Teaching and testing

Many language teachers harbour a deep mistrust of tests and of testers. The starting point for this book is the admission that this mistrust is frequently well-founded. It cannot be denied that a great deal of language testing is of very poor quality. Too often language tests have a harmful effect on teaching and learning; and too often they fail to measure accurately whatever it is they are intended to measure.

Backwash

The effect of testing on teaching and learning is known as *backwash*. Backwash can be harmful or beneficial. If a test is regarded as important, then preparation for it can come to dominate all teaching and learning activities. And if the test content and testing techniques are at variance with the objectives of the course, then there is likely to be harmful backwash. An instance of this would be where students are following an English course which is meant to train them in the language skills (including writing) necessary for university study in an English-speaking country, but where the language test which they have to take in order to be admitted to a university does not test those skills directly. If the skill of writing, for example, is tested only by multiple choice items, then there is great pressure to practise such items rather than practise the skill of writing itself. This is clearly undesirable.

We have just looked at a case of harmful backwash. However, backwash need not always be harmful; indeed it can be positively beneficial. I was once involved in the development of an English language test for an English medium university in a non-English-speaking country. The test was to be administered at the end of an intensive year of English study there and would be used to determine which students would be allowed to go on to their undergraduate courses (taught in English) and which would have to leave the university. A test was devised which was based directly on an analysis of the English language needs of first year undergraduate students, and which included tasks as similar as possible to those which they would have to perform as undergraduates (reading textbook materials, taking notes during lectures, and so on). The introduction of this test, in place of one which had been entirely multiple choice, had an immediate effect on teaching: the syllabus was redesigned, new books were chosen, classes were conducted differently. The result of these changes was that by the end of their year's training, in circumstances made particularly difficult by greatly increased numbers and limited resources, the students reached a much higher standard in English than had ever been achieved in the university's history. This was a case of *beneficial* backwash.

Davies (1968:5) has said that 'the good test is an obedient servant since it follows and apes the teaching'. I find it difficult to agree. The proper relationship between teaching and testing is surely that of partnership. It is true that there may be occasions when the teaching is good and appropriate and the testing is not; we are then likely to suffer from harmful backwash. This would seem to be the situation that leads Davies to confine testing to the role of servant of teaching. But equally there may be occasions when teaching is poor or inappropriate and when testing is able to exert a beneficial influence. We cannot expect testing only to follow teaching. What we should demand of it, however, is that it should be supportive of good teaching and, where necessary, exert a corrective influence on bad teaching. If testing always had a beneficial backwash on teaching, it would have a much better reputation amongst teachers. Chapter 6 of this book is devoted to a discussion of how beneficial backwash can be achieved.

Inaccurate tests

The second reason for mistrusting tests is that very often they fail to measure accurately whatever it is that they are intended to measure. Teachers know this. Students' true abilities are not always reflected in the test scores that they obtain. To a certain extent this is inevitable. Language abilities are not easy to measure; we cannot expect a level of accuracy comparable to those of measurements in the physical sciences. But we can expect greater accuracy than is frequently achieved.

Why are tests inaccurate? The causes of inaccuracy (and ways of minimising their effects) are identified and discussed in subsequent chapters, but a short answer is possible here. There are two main sources of inaccuracy. The first of these concerns test content and techniques. To return to an earlier example, if we want to know how well someone can write, there is absolutely no way we can get a really accurate measure of their ability by means of a multiple choice test. Professional testers have expended great effort, and not a little money, in attempts to do it; but they have always failed. We may be able to get an approximate measure, but that is all. When testing is carried out on a very large scale, when the scoring of tens of thousands of compositions might seem not to be a practical proposition, it is understandable that potentially greater accuracy is sacrificed for reasons of economy and convenience. But it does not give testing a good name! And it does set a bad example.

While few teachers would wish to follow that particular example in order to test writing ability, the overwhelming practice in large-scale testing of using multiple choice items does lead to imitation in circumstances where such items are not at all appropriate. What is more, the imitation tends to be of a very poor standard. Good multiple choice items are notoriously difficult to write. A great deal of time and effort has to go into their construction. Too many multiple choice tests are written where such care and attention is not given (and indeed may not be possible). The result is a set of poor items that cannot possibly provide accurate measurements. One of the principal aims of this book is to discourage the use of inappropriate techniques and to show that teacher-made tests can be superior in certain respects to their professional counterparts.

The second source of inaccuracy is lack of *reliability*. Reliability is a technical term which is explained in Chapter 5. For the moment it is enough to say that a test is reliable if it measures consistently. On a reliable test you can be confident that someone will get more or less the same score, whether they happen to take it on one particular day or on the next; whereas on an unreliable test the score is quite likely to be considerably different, depending on the day on which it is taken.

Unreliability has two origins: features of the test itself, and the way it is scored. In the first case, something about the test creates a tendency for individuals to perform significantly differently on different occasions when they might take the test. Their performance might be quite different if they took the test on, say, Wednesday rather than on the following day. As a result, even if the *scoring* of their performance on the test is perfectly accurate (that is, the scorers do not make any mistakes), they will nevertheless obtain a markedly different score, depending on when they actually sat the test, even though there has been no change in the ability which the test is meant to measure. This is not the place to list all possible features of a test which might make it unreliable, but examples are: unclear instructions, ambiguous questions, items that result in guessing on the part of the test takers. While it is not possible entirely to eliminate such differences in behaviour from one test administration to another (human beings are not machines), there *are* principles of test construction which can reduce them.

In the second case, equivalent test performances are accorded significantly different scores. For example, the same composition may be given very different scores by different markers (or even by the same marker on different occasions). Fortunately, there are well-understood ways of minimising such differences in scoring.

Most (but not all) large testing organisations, to their credit, take every precaution to make their tests, and the scoring of them, as reliable as possible, and are generally highly successful in this respect. Small-scale testing, on the other hand, tends to be less reliable than it should be. Another aim of this book, then, is to show how to achieve greater reliability in testing. Advice on this is to be found in Chapter 5.

The need for tests

So far this chapter has been concerned to understand why tests are so mistrusted by many language teachers. We have seen that this mistrust is often justified. One conclusion drawn from this might be that we would be better off without language tests. Teaching is, after all, the primary activity; if testing comes in conflict with it, then it is testing which should go, especially when it has been admitted that so much testing provides inaccurate information. This is a plausible argument – but there are other considerations, which might lead to a different conclusion.

Information about people's language ability is often very useful and sometimes necessary. It is difficult to imagine, for example, British and American universities accepting students from overseas without some knowledge of their proficiency in English. The same is true for organisations hiring interpreters or translators. They certainly need dependable measures of language ability.

Within teaching systems, too, as long as it is thought appropriate for individuals to be given a statement of what they have achieved in a second or foreign language, then tests of some kind or other will be needed.[1] They will also be needed in order to provide information about the achievement of groups of learners, without which it is difficult to see how rational educational decisions can be made. While for some purposes teachers' assessments of their own students are both appropriate and sufficient, this is not true for the cases just mentioned. Even without considering the possibility of bias, we have to recognise the need for a common yardstick, which tests provide, in order to make meaningful comparisons.

If it is accepted that tests are necessary, and if we care about testing and its effect on teaching and learning, the other conclusion (in my view, the correct one) to be drawn from a recognition of the poor quality of so much testing is that we should do everything that we can to improve the practice of testing.

---

1. It will become clear that in this book the word 'test' is interpreted widely. It is used to refer to any structured attempt to measure language ability. No distinction is made between 'examination' and 'test'.

What is to be done?

The teaching profession can make two contributions to the improvement of testing: they can write better tests themselves, and they can put pressure on others, including professional testers and examining boards, to improve *their* tests. This book represents an attempt to help them do both.

For the reader who doubts that teachers can influence the large testing institutions, let this chapter end with a further reference to the testing of writing through multiple choice items. This was the practice followed by those responsible for TOEFL (Test of English as a Foreign Language), the test taken by most non-native speakers of English applying to North American universities. Over a period of many years they maintained that it was simply not possible to test the writing ability of hundreds of thousands of candidates by means of a composition: it was impracticable and the results, anyhow, would be unreliable. Yet in 1986 a writing test (Test of Written English), in which candidates actually have to write for thirty minutes, was introduced as a supplement to TOEFL, and already many colleges in the United States are requiring applicants to take this test in addition to TOEFL. The principal reason given for this change was pressure from English language teachers who had finally convinced those responsible for the TOEFL of the overriding need for a writing task which would provide beneficial backwash.

READER ACTIVITIES

1. Think of tests with which you are familiar (the tests may be inter-national or local, written by professionals or by teachers). What do you think the backwash effect of each of them is? Harmful or beneficial? What are your reasons for coming to these conclusions?
2. Consider these tests again. Do you think that they give accurate or inaccurate information? What are your reasons for coming to these conclusions?

Further reading

For an account of how the introduction of a new test can have a striking beneficial effect on teaching and learning, see Hughes (1988a). For a review of the new TOEFL writing test which acknowledges its potential beneficial backwash effect but which also points out that the narrow range of writing tasks set (they are of only two types) may result in narrow training in writing, see Greenberg (1986). For a discussion of the ethics of language testing, see Spolsky (1981).

2 Testing as problem solving: an overview of the book

The purpose of this chapter is to introduce readers to the idea of testing as problem solving and to show how the content and structure of the book are designed to help them to become successful solvers of testing problems.

Language testers are sometimes asked to say what is 'the best test' or 'the best testing technique'. Such questions reveal a misunderstanding of what is involved in the practice of language testing. In fact there is no best test or best technique. A test which proves ideal for one purpose may be quite useless for another; a technique which may work very well in one situation can be entirely inappropriate in another. As we saw in the previous chapter, what suits large testing corporations may be quite out of place in the tests of teaching institutions. In the same way, two teaching institutions may require very different tests, depending amongst other things on the objectives of their courses, the purpose and importance of the tests, and the resources that are available. The assumption that has to be made therefore is that each testing situation is unique and so sets a particular testing problem. It is the tester's job to provide the best solution to that problem. The aims of this book are to equip readers with the basic knowledge and techniques first to solve such problems, secondly to evaluate the solutions proposed or already implemented by others, and thirdly to argue persuasively for improvements in testing practice where these seem necessary.

In every situation the first step must be to state the testing problem as clearly as possible. Without a clear statement of the problem it is hard to arrive at the right solution. Every testing problem can be expressed in the same general terms: we want to create a test or testing system which will:

consistently provide accurate measures of precisely the abilities[1] in which we are interested;

have a beneficial effect on teaching (in those cases where the tests are likely to influence teaching);

be economical in terms of time and money.

---

1. 'Abilities' is not being used here in any technical sense. It refers simply to what people can do in, or with, a language. It could, for example, include the ability to converse fluently in a language, as well as the ability to recite grammatical rules (if that is something which we are interested in measuring!). It does not, however, refer to

Let us describe the general testing problem in a little more detail. The first thing that testers have to be clear about is the purpose of testing in any particular situation. Different purposes will usually require different kinds of tests. This may seem obvious but it is something which seems not always to be recognised. The purposes of testing discussed in this book are:

- to measure language proficiency regardless of any language courses that candidates may have followed
- to discover how far students have achieved the objectives of a course of study
- to diagnose students' strengths and weaknesses, to identify what they know and what they do not know
- to assist placement of students by identifying the stage or part of a teaching programme most appropriate to their ability

All of these purposes are discussed in the next chapter. That chapter also introduces different kinds of testing and test techniques: direct as opposed to indirect testing; discrete-point versus integrative testing; criterion-referenced testing as against norm-referenced testing; objective and subjective testing.

In stating the testing problem in general terms above, we spoke of providing consistent measures of precisely the abilities we are interested in. A test which does this is said to be '*valid*'. Chapter 4 addresses itself to various kinds of validity. It provides advice on the achievement of validity in test construction and shows how validity is measured.

The word 'consistently' was used in the statement of the testing problem. The consistency with which accurate measurements are made is in fact an essential ingredient of validity. If a test measures consistently (if, for example a person's score on the test is likely to be very similar regardless of whether they happen to take it on, say, Monday morning rather than on Tuesday afternoon, assuming that there has been no significant change in their ability) it is said to be *reliable*. Reliability, already referred to in the previous chapter, is an absolutely essential quality of tests – what use is a test if it will give widely differing estimates of an individual's (unchanged) ability? – yet it is something which is distinctly lacking in very many teacher-made tests. Chapter 5 gives advice on how to achieve reliability and explains the ways in which it is measured.

The concept of backwash effect was introduced in the previous chapter. Chapter 6 identifies a number of conditions for tests to meet in order to *achieve beneficial backwash*.

language aptitude, the talent which people have, in differing degrees, for learning languages. The measurement of this talent in order to predict how well or how quickly individuals will learn a foreign language, is beyond the scope of this book. The interested reader is referred to Pimsleur (1968), Carroll (1981), and Skehan (1986).

All tests cost time and money – to prepare, administer, score and interpret. Time and money are in limited supply, and so there is often likely to be a conflict between what appears to be a perfect testing solution in a particular situation and considerations of *practicality*. This issue is also discussed in Chapter 6.

To rephrase the general testing problem identified above: the basic problem is to develop tests which are valid and reliable, which have a beneficial backwash effect on teaching (where this is relevant), and which are practical. The next four chapters of the book are intended to look more closely at the relevant concepts and so help the reader to formulate such problems clearly in particular instances, and to provide advice on how to approach their solution.

The second half of the book is devoted to more detailed advice on the construction and use of tests, the putting into practice of the principles outlined in earlier chapters. Chapter 7 outlines and exemplifies the various stages of test construction. Chapter 8 discusses a number of *testing techniques*. Chapters 9–13 show how a variety of language abilities can best be tested, particularly within teaching institutions. Chapter 14 gives straightforward advice on the administration of tests.

We have to say something about statistics. Some understanding of statistics is useful, indeed necessary, for a proper appreciation of testing matters and for successful problem solving. At the same time, we have to recognise that there is a limit to what many readers will be prepared to do, especially if they are at all afraid of mathematics. For this reason, statistical matters are kept to a minimum and are presented in terms that everyone should be able to grasp. The emphasis will be on *interpretation* rather than on calculation. For the more adventurous reader, however, Appendix 1 explains how to carry out a number of statistical operations.

Further reading

The collection of critical reviews of nearly 50 English language tests (mostly British and American), edited by Alderson, Krahnke and Stansfield (1987), reveals how well professional test writers are thought to have solved *their* problems. A full understanding of the reviews will depend to some degree on an assimilation of the content of Chapters 3, 4, and 5 of this book.

3 Kinds of test and testing

This chapter begins by considering the purposes for which language testing is carried out. It goes on to make a number of distinctions: between direct and indirect testing, between discrete point and integrative testing, between norm-referenced and criterion-referenced testing, and between objective and subjective testing. Finally there is a note on communicative language testing.

We use tests to obtain information. The information that we hope to obtain will of course vary from situation to situation. It is possible, nevertheless, to categorise tests according to a small number of *kinds* of information being sought. This categorisation will prove useful both in deciding whether an existing test is suitable for a particular purpose and in writing appropriate new tests where these are necessary. The four types of test which we will discuss in the following sections are: proficiency tests, achievement tests, diagnostic tests, and placement tests.

Proficiency tests

Proficiency tests are designed to measure people's ability in a language regardless of any training they may have had in that language. The content of a proficiency test, therefore, is not based on the content or objectives of language courses which people taking the test may have followed. Rather, it is based on a specification of what candidates have to be able to do in the language in order to be considered proficient. This raises the question of what we mean by the word 'proficient'.

In the case of some proficiency tests, 'proficient' means having sufficient command of the language *for a particular purpose*. An example of this would be a test designed to discover whether someone can function successfully as a United Nations translator. Another example would be a test used to determine whether a student's English is good enough to follow a course of study at a British university. Such a test may even attempt to take into account the level and kind of English needed to follow courses in particular subject areas. It might, for example, have one form of the test for arts subjects, another for sciences, and so on. Whatever the particular purpose to which the language is to be put, this will be reflected in the specification of test content at an early stage of a test's development.

There are other proficiency tests which, by contrast, do not have any occupation or course of study in mind. For them the concept of proficiency is more general. British examples of these would be the Cambridge examinations (First Certificate Examination and Proficiency Examination) and the Oxford EFL examinations (Preliminary and Higher). The function of these tests is to show whether candidates have reached a certain standard with respect to certain specified abilities. Such examining bodies are independent of the teaching institutions and so can be relied on by potential employers etc. to make fair comparisons between candidates from different institutions and different countries. Though there is no particular purpose in mind for the language, these general proficiency tests should have detailed specifications saying just what it is that successful candidates will have demonstrated that they can do. Each test should be seen to be based directly on these specifications. All users of a test (teachers, students, employers, etc.) can then judge whether the test is suitable for them, and can interpret test results. It is not enough to have some vague notion of proficiency, however prestigious the testing body concerned.

Despite differences between them of content and level of difficulty, all proficiency tests have in common the fact that they are not based on courses that candidates may have previously taken. On the other hand, as we saw in Chapter 1, such tests may themselves exercise considerable influence over the method and content of language courses. Their backwash effect – for this is what it is – may be beneficial or harmful. In my view, the effect of *some* widely used proficiency tests is more harmful than beneficial. However, the teachers of students who take such tests, and whose work suffers from a harmful backwash effect, may be able to exercise more influence over the testing organisations concerned than they realise. The recent addition to TOEFL, referred to in Chapter 1, is a case in point.

Achievement tests

Most teachers are unlikely to be responsible for proficiency tests. It is much more probable that they will be involved in the preparation and use of achievement tests. In contrast to proficiency tests, achievement tests are directly related to language courses, their purpose being to establish how successful individual students, groups of students, or the courses themselves have been in achieving objectives. They are of two kinds: *final* achievement tests and *progress* achievement tests.

Final achievement tests are those administered at the end of a course of study. They may be written and administered by ministries of education, official examining boards, or by members of teaching institutions. Clearly the content of these tests must be related to the courses with which they are concerned, but the nature of this relationship is a matter of disagreement amongst language testers.

In the view of some testers, the content of a final achievement test should be based directly on a detailed course syllabus or on the books and other materials used. This has been referred to as the 'syllabus-content approach'. It has an obvious appeal, since the test only contains what it is thought that the students have actually encountered, and thus can be considered, in this respect at least, a fair test. The disadvantage is that if the syllabus is badly designed, or the books and other materials are badly chosen, then the results of a test can be very misleading. Successful performance on the test may not truly indicate successful achievement of course objectives. For example, a course may have as an *objective* the development of conversational ability, but the course itself and the test may require students only to utter carefully prepared statements about their home town, the weather, or whatever. Another course may aim to develop a reading ability in German, but the test may limit itself to the vocabulary the students are known to have met. Yet another course is intended to prepare students for university study in English, but the syllabus (and so the course and the test) may not include listening (with note taking) to English delivered in lecture style on topics of the kind that the students will have to deal with at university. In each of these examples – all of them based on actual cases – test results will fail to show what students have achieved in terms of course objectives.

The alternative approach is to base the test content directly on the objectives of the course. This has a number of advantages. First, it compels course designers to be explicit about objectives. Secondly, it makes it possible for performance on the test to show just how far students have achieved those objectives. This in turn puts pressure on those responsible for the syllabus and for the selection of books and materials to ensure that these are consistent with the course objectives. Tests based on objectives work against the perpetuation of poor teaching practice, something which course-content-based tests, almost as if part of a conspiracy, fail to do. It is my belief that to base test content on course objectives is much to be preferred: it will provide more accurate information about individual and group achievement, and it is likely to promote a more beneficial backwash effect on teaching.[1]

---

1. Of course, if objectives are unrealistic, then tests will also reveal a failure to achieve them. This too can only be regarded as salutary. There may be disagreement as to why there has been a failure to achieve the objectives, but at least this provides a starting point for necessary discussion which otherwise might never have taken place.

Now it might be argued that to base test content on objectives rather than on course content is unfair to students. If the course content does not fit well with objectives, they will be expected to do things for which they have not been prepared. In a sense this is true. But in another sense it is not. If a test is based on the content of a poor or inappropriate course, the students taking it will be misled as to the extent of their achievement and the quality of the course. Whereas if the test is based on objectives, not only will the information it gives be more useful, but there is less chance of the course surviving in its present unsatisfactory form. Initially some students may suffer, but future students will benefit from the pressure for change. The long-term interests of students are best served by final achievement tests whose content is based on course objectives.

The reader may wonder at this stage whether there is any real difference between final achievement tests and proficiency tests. If a test is based on the objectives of a course, and these are equivalent to the language needs on which a proficiency test is based, then there is no reason to expect a difference between the form and content of the two tests. Two things have to be remembered, however. First, objectives and needs will not typically coincide in this way. Secondly, many achievement tests are not in fact based on course objectives. These facts have implications both for the users of test results and for test writers. Test users have to know on what basis an achievement test has been constructed, and be aware of the possibly limited validity and applicability of test scores. Test writers, on the other hand, must create achievement tests which reflect the objectives of a particular course, and not expect a general proficiency test (or some imitation of it) to provide a satisfactory alternative.

Progress achievement tests, as their name suggests, are intended to measure the progress that students are making. Since 'progress' is towards the achievement of course objectives, these tests too should relate to objectives. But how? One way of measuring progress would be repeatedly to administer final achievement tests, the (hopefully) increasing scores indicating the progress made. This is not really feasible, particularly in the early stages of a course. The low scores obtained would be discouraging to students and quite possibly to their teachers. The alternative is to establish a series of well-defined short-term objectives. These should make a clear progression towards the final achievement test based on course objectives. Then if the syllabus and teaching are appropriate to these objectives, progress tests based on short-term objectives will fit well with what has been taught. If not, there will be pressure to create a better fit. If it is the syllabus that is at fault, it is the tester's responsibility to make clear that it is *there* that change is needed, not in the tests.

In addition to more formal achievement tests which require careful preparation, teachers should feel free to set their own 'pop quizzes'. These serve both to make a rough check on students' progress and to keep students on their toes. Since such tests will not form part of formal assessment procedures, their construction and scoring need not be too rigorous. Nevertheless, they should be seen as measuring progress towards the intermediate objectives on which the more formal progress achievement tests are based. They can, however, reflect the particular 'route' that an individual teacher is taking towards the achievement of objectives.

It has been argued in this section that it is better to base the content of achievement tests on course objectives rather than on the detailed content of a course. However, it may not be at all easy to convince colleagues of this, especially if the latter approach is already being followed. Not only is there likely to be natural resistance to change, but such a change may represent a threat to many people. A great deal of skill, tact and, possibly, political manoeuvring may be called for – topics on which this book cannot pretend to give advice.

Diagnostic tests

Diagnostic tests are used to identify students' strengths and weaknesses. They are intended primarily to ascertain what further teaching is necessary. At the level of broad language skills this is reasonably straightforward. We can be fairly confident of our ability to create tests that will tell us that a student is particularly weak in, say, speaking as opposed to reading in a language. Indeed existing proficiency tests may often prove adequate for this purpose.

We may be able to go further, analysing samples of a student's performance in writing or speaking in order to create profiles of the student's ability with respect to such categories as 'grammatical accuracy' or 'linguistic appropriacy'. (See Chapter 9 for a scoring system that may provide such an analysis.)

But it is not so easy to obtain a detailed analysis of a student's command of grammatical structures, something which would tell us, for example, whether she or he had mastered the present perfect/past tense distinction in English. In order to be sure of this, we would need a number of examples of the choice the student made between the two structures in every different context which we thought was significantly different and important enough to warrant obtaining information on. A single example of each would not be enough, since a student might give the correct response by chance. As a result, a comprehensive diagnostic test of English grammar would be vast (think of what would be involved in testing the modal verbs, for instance). The size of such a test would make it impractical to administer in a routine fashion. For this reason, very few tests are constructed for purely diagnostic purposes, and those that there are do not provide very detailed information.

The lack of good diagnostic tests is unfortunate. They could be extremely useful for individualised instruction or self-instruction. Learners would be shown where gaps exist in their command of the language, and could be directed to sources of information, exemplification and practice. Happily, the ready availability of relatively inexpensive computers with very large memories may change the situation. Well-written computer programmes would ensure that the learner spent no more time than was absolutely necessary to obtain the desired information, and without the need for a test administrator. Tests of this kind will still need a tremendous amount of work to produce. Whether or not they become generally available will depend on the willingness of individuals to write them and of publishers to distribute them.

Placement tests

Placement tests, as their name suggests, are intended to provide information which will help to place students at the stage (or in the part) of the teaching programme most appropriate to their abilities. Typically they are used to assign students to classes at different levels.

Placement tests can be bought, but this is not to be recommended unless the institution concerned is quite sure that the test being considered suits its particular teaching programme. No one placement test will work for every institution, and the initial assumption about any test that is commercially available must be that it will not work well.

The placement tests which are most successful are those constructed for particular situations. They depend on the identification of the key features at different levels of teaching in the institution. They are tailor-made rather than bought off the peg. This usually means that they have been produced 'in house'. The work that goes into their construction is rewarded by the saving in time and effort through accurate placement. An example of how a placement test might be designed within an institution is given in Chapter 7; the validation of placement tests is referred to in Chapter 4.

Direct versus indirect testing

So far in this chapter we have considered a number of uses to which test results are put. We now distinguish between two approaches to test construction.

Testing is said to be *direct* when it requires the candidate to perform precisely the skill which we wish to measure. If we want to know how well candidates can write compositions, we get them to write compositions. If we want to know how well they pronounce a language, we get them to speak. The tasks, and the texts which are used, should be as authentic as possible. The fact that candidates are aware that they are in a test situation means that the tasks cannot be really authentic. Nevertheless the effort is made to make them as realistic as possible.

Direct testing is easier to carry out when it is intended to measure the productive skills of speaking and writing. The very acts of speaking and writing provide us with information about the candidate's ability. With listening and reading, however, it is necessary to get candidates not only to listen or read but also to demonstrate that they have done this successfully. The tester has to devise methods of eliciting such evidence accurately and without the method interfering with the performance of the skills in which he or she is interested. Appropriate methods for achieving this are discussed in Chapters 11 and 12. Interestingly enough, in many texts on language testing it is the testing of productive skills that is presented as being most problematic, for reasons usually connected with reliability. In fact the problems are by no means insurmountable, as we shall see in Chapters 9 and 10.

Direct testing has a number of attractions. First, provided that we are clear about just what abilities we want to assess, it is relatively straightforward to create the conditions which will elicit the behaviour on which to base our judgements. Secondly, at least in the case of the productive skills, the assessment and interpretation of students' performance is also quite straightforward. Thirdly, since practice for the test involves practice of the skills that we wish to foster, there is likely to be a helpful backwash effect.

Indirect testing attempts to measure the abilities which *underlie* the skills in which we are interested. One section of the TOEFL, for example, was developed as an indirect measure of writing ability. It contains items of the following kind:

> At first the old woman seemed unwilling to accept anything that was offered her by my friend and I.

where the candidate has to identify which of the underlined elements is erroneous or inappropriate in formal standard English. While the ability to respond to such items has been shown to be related statistically to the ability to write compositions (though the strength of the relationship was not particularly great), it is clearly not the same thing. Another example of indirect testing is Lado's (1961) proposed method of testing pronunciation ability by a paper and pencil test in which the candidate has to identify pairs of words which rhyme with each other.

Perhaps the main appeal of indirect testing is that it seems to offer the possibility of testing a representative sample of a finite number of abilities which underlie a potentially indefinitely large number of manifestations of them. If, for example, we take a representative sample of grammatical structures, then, it may be argued, we have taken a sample which is relevant for *all* the situations in which control of grammar is necessary. By contrast, direct testing is inevitably limited to a rather small sample of *tasks*, which may call on a restricted and possibly unrepresentative range of grammatical structures. On this argument, indirect testing is superior to direct testing in that its results are more generalisable.

The main problem with indirect tests is that the relationship between performance on them and performance of the skills in which we are usually more interested tends to be rather weak in strength and uncertain in nature. We do not yet know enough about the component parts of, say, composition writing to predict accurately composition writing ability from scores on tests which measure the abilities which we *believe* underlie it. We may construct tests of grammar, vocabulary, discourse markers, handwriting, punctuation, and what we will. But we still will not be able to predict accurately scores on compositions (even if we make sure of the representativeness of the composition scores by taking many samples).

It seems to me that in our present state of knowledge, at least as far as proficiency and final achievement tests are concerned, it is preferable to concentrate on direct testing. Provided that we sample reasonably widely (for example require at least two compositions, each calling for a different kind of writing and on a different topic), we can expect more accurate estimates of the abilities that really concern us than would be obtained through indirect testing. The fact that direct tests are generally easier to construct simply reinforces this view with respect to institutional tests, as does their greater potential for beneficial backwash. It is only fair to say, however, that many testers are reluctant to commit themselves entirely to direct testing and will always include an indirect element in their tests. Of course, to obtain diagnostic information on underlying abilities, such as control of particular grammatical structures, indirect testing is called for.

Discrete point versus integrative testing

Discrete point testing refers to the testing of one element at a time, item by item. This might involve, for example, a series of items each testing a particular grammatical structure. Integrative testing, by contrast, requires the candidate to combine many language elements in the completion of a task. This might involve writing a composition, making notes while listening to a lecture, taking a dictation, or completing a cloze passage. Clearly this distinction is not unrelated to that between indirect and direct testing. Discrete point tests will almost always be indirect, while integrative tests will tend to be direct. However, some integrative testing methods, such as the cloze procedure, are indirect.

Norm-referenced versus criterion-referenced testing

Imagine that a reading test is administered to an individual student. When we ask how the student performed on the test, we may be given two kinds of answer. An answer of the first kind would be that the student obtained a score that placed her or him in the top ten per cent of candidates who have taken that test, or in the bottom five per cent; or that she or he did better than sixty per cent of those who took it. A test which is designed to give this kind of information is said to be *norm-referenced*. It relates one candidate's performance to that of other candidates. We are not told directly what the student is capable of doing in the language.

The other kind of answer we might be given is exemplified by the following, taken from the Interagency Language Roundtable (ILR) language skill level descriptions for reading:

> **Sufficient comprehension to read simple, authentic written materials in a form equivalent to usual printing or typescript on subjects within a familiar context.** Able to read with some misunderstandings straightforward, familiar, factual material, but in general insufficiently experienced with the language to draw inferences directly from the linguistic aspects of the text. Can locate and understand the main ideas and details in materials written for the general reader ... The individual can read uncomplicated, but authentic prose on familiar subjects that are normally presented in a predictable sequence which aids the reader in understanding. Texts may include descriptions and narrations in contexts such as news items describing frequently-occurring events, simple biographical information, social notices, formulaic business letters, and simple technical information written for the general reader. Generally the prose that can be read by the individual is predominantly in straightforward/high-frequency sentence patterns. The individual does not have a broad active vocabulary ... but is able to use contextual and real-world clues to understand the text.

Similarly, a candidate who is awarded the Berkshire Certificate of Proficiency in German Level 1 can 'speak and react to others using simple language in the following contexts':

- to greet, interact with and take leave of others;
- to exchange information on personal background, home, school life and interests;

17

- to discuss and make choices, decisions and plans;
- to express opinions, make requests and suggestions;
- to ask for information and understand instructions.

In these two cases we learn nothing about how the individual's performance compares with that of other candidates. Rather we learn something about what he or she can actually do in the language. Tests which are designed to provide this kind of information *directly* are said to be *criterion-referenced*.[2]

The purpose of criterion-referenced tests is to classify people according to whether or not they are able to perform some task or set of tasks satisfactorily. The tasks are set, and the performances are evaluated. It does not matter in principle whether all the candidates are successful, or none of the candidates is successful. The tasks are set, and those who perform them satisfactorily 'pass'; those who don't, 'fail'. This means that students are encouraged to measure their progress in relation to meaningful criteria, without feeling that, because they are less able than most of their fellows, they are destined to fail. In the case of the Berkshire German Certificate, for example, it is hoped that all students who are entered for it will be successful. Criterion-referenced tests therefore have two positive virtues: they set standards meaningful in terms of what people can *do*, which do not change with different groups of candidates; and they motivate students to attain those standards.

The need for direct interpretation of performance means that the construction of a criterion-referenced test may be quite different from that of a norm-referenced test designed to serve the same purpose. Let us imagine that the purpose is to assess the English language ability of students in relation to the demands made by English medium universities. The criterion-referenced test would almost certainly have to be based on an analysis of what students had to be able to do with or through English at university. Tasks would then be set similar to those to be met at university. If this were not done, direct interpretation of performance would be impossible. The norm-referenced test, on the other hand, while its content might be based on a similar analysis, is not so restricted. The Michigan Test of English Language Proficiency, for instance, has multiple choice grammar, vocabulary, and reading comprehension components. A candidate's score on the test does not tell us directly what his or her English ability is in relation to the demands that would be made on it at an English-medium university. To know this, we must consult a table which makes recommendations as to the academic load that a student

2. People differ somewhat in their use of the term 'criterion-referenced'. This is unimportant provided that the sense intended is made clear. The sense in which it is used here is the one which I feel will be most useful to the reader in analysing testing problems.

with that score should be allowed to carry, this being based on experience over the years of students with similar scores, not on any meaning in the score itself. In the same way, university administrators have learned from experience how to interpret TOEFL scores and to set minimum scores for their own institutions.

Books on language testing have tended to give advice which is more appropriate to norm-referenced testing than to criterion-referenced testing. One reason for this may be that procedures for use with norm-referenced tests (particularly with respect to such matters as the analysis of items and the estimation of reliability) are well established, while those for criterion-referenced tests are not. The view taken in this book, and argued for in Chapter 6, is that criterion-referenced tests are often to be preferred, not least for the beneficial backwash effect they are likely to have. The lack of agreed procedures for such tests is not sufficient reason for them to be excluded from consideration.

Objective testing versus subjective testing

The distinction here is between methods of *scoring*, and nothing else. If no judgement is required on the part of the scorer, then the scoring is objective. A multiple choice test, with the correct responses unambiguously identified, would be a case in point. If judgement is called for, the scoring is said to be subjective. There are different degrees of subjectivity in testing. The impressionistic scoring of a composition may be considered more subjective than the scoring of short answers in response to questions on a reading passage.

Objectivity in scoring is sought after by many testers, not for itself, but for the greater reliability it brings. In general, the less subjective the scoring, the greater agreement there will be between two different scorers (and between the scores of one person scoring the same test paper on different occasions). However, there are ways of obtaining reliable subjective scoring, even of compositions. These are discussed first in Chapter 5.

Communicative language testing

Much has been written in recent years about 'communicative language testing'. Discussions have centred on the desirability of measuring the ability to take part in acts of communication (including reading and listening) and on the best way to do this. It is assumed in this book that it is usually communicative ability which we want to test. As a result, what I believe to be the most significant points made in discussions of communi-

cative testing are to be found throughout. A recapitulation under a
separate heading would therefore be redundant.

READER ACTIVITIES

Consider a number of language tests with which you are familiar. For
each of them, answer the following questions:

1. What is the purpose of the test?
2. Does it represent direct or indirect testing (or a mixture of both)?
3. Are the items discrete point or integrative (or a mixture of both)?
4. Which items are objective, and which are subjective? Can you order
   the subjective items according to degree of subjectivity?
5. Is the test norm-referenced or criterion-referenced?
6. Does the test measure communicative abilities? Would you describe it
   as a communicative test? Justify your answers.
7. What relationship is there between the answers to question 6 and the
   answers to the other questions?

Further reading

For a discussion of the two approaches towards achievement test content
specification, see Pilliner (1968). Alderson (1987) reports on research
into the possible contributions of the computer to language testing.
Direct testing calls for texts and tasks to be as authentic as possible: Vol.
2, No. 1 (1985) of the journal *Language Testing* is devoted to articles on
authenticity in language testing. An account of the development of an
indirect test of writing is given in Godshalk *et al.* (1966). Classic short
papers on criterion-referencing and norm-referencing (not restricted to
language testing) are by Popham (1978), favouring criterion-referenced
testing, and Ebel (1978), arguing for the superiority of norm-referenced
testing. The description of reading ability given in this chapter comes
from the Interagency Language Roundtable Language Skill Level
Descriptions. Comparable descriptions at a number of levels for the four
skills, intended for assessing students in academic contexts, have been
devised by the American Council for the teaching of Foreign Languages
(ACTFL). These ACTFL Guidelines are available from ACTFL at 579
Broadway, Hastings-on-Hudson, NY 10706, USA. It should be said,
however, that the form that these take and the way in which they were
constructed have been the subject of some controversy. Doubts about the
applicability of criterion-referencing to language testing are expressed by
Skehan (1984); for a different view, see Hughes (1986). Carroll (1961)

made the distinction between discrete point and integrative language testing. Oller (1979) discusses integrative testing techniques. Morrow (1979) is a seminal paper on communicative language testing. Further discussion of the topic is to be found in Canale and Swain (1980), Alderson and Hughes (1981, Part 1), Hughes and Porter (1983), and Davies (1988). Weir's (1988a) book has as its title *Communicative language testing*.

4 Validity

We already know from Chapter 2 that a test is said to be valid if it measures accurately what it is intended to measure. This seems simple enough. When closely examined, however, the concept of validity reveals a number of aspects, each of which deserves our attention. This chapter will present each aspect in turn, and attempt to show its relevance for the solution of language testing problems.

Content validity

A test is said to have content validity if its content constitutes a representative sample of the language skills, structures, etc. with which it is meant to be concerned. It is obvious that a grammar test, for instance, must be made up of items testing knowledge or control of grammar. But this in itself does not ensure content validity. The test would have content validity only if it included a proper sample of the *relevant* structures. Just what are the relevant structures will depend, of course, upon the purpose of the test. We would not expect an achievement test for intermediate learners to contain just the same set of structures as one for advanced learners. In order to judge whether or not a test has content validity, we need a *specification* of the skills or structures etc. that it is meant to cover. Such a specification should be made at a very early stage in test construction. It isn't to be expected that everything in the specification will always appear in the test; there may simply be too many things for all of them to appear in a single test. But it will provide the test constructor with the basis for making a principled selection of elements for inclusion in the test. A comparison of test specification and test content is the basis for judgements as to content validity. Ideally these judgements should be made by people who are familiar with language teaching and testing but who are not directly concerned with the production of the test in question.

What is the importance of content validity? First, the greater a test's content validity, the more likely it is to be an accurate measure of what it is supposed to measure. A test in which major areas identified in the specification are under-represented – or not represented at all – is unlikely to be accurate. Secondly, such a test is likely to have a harmful backwash effect. Areas which are not tested are likely to become areas ignored in teaching and learning. Too often the content of tests is determined by what is *easy* to test rather than what is *important* to test. The best safeguard against this is to write full test specifications and to ensure that the test content is a fair reflection of these. Advice on the writing of specifications and on the judgement of content validity is to be found in Chapter 7.

Criterion-related validity

Another approach to test validity is to see how far results on the test agree with those provided by some independent and highly dependable assessment of the candidate's ability. This independent assessment is thus the criterion measure against which the test is validated.

There are essentially two kinds of criterion-related validity: concurrent validity and predictive validity. *Concurrent validity* is established when the test and the criterion are administered at about the same time. To exemplify this kind of validation in achievement testing, let us consider a situation where course objectives call for an oral component as part of the final achievement test. The objectives may list a large number of 'functions' which students are expected to perform orally, to test all of which might take 45 minutes for each student. This could well be impractical. Perhaps it is felt that only ten minutes can be devoted to each student for the oral component. The question then arises: can such a ten-minute session give a sufficiently accurate estimate of the student's ability with respect to the functions specified in the course objectives? Is it, in other words, a valid measure?

From the point of view of content validity, this will depend on how many of the functions are tested in the component, and how representative they are of the complete set of functions included in the objectives. Every effort should be made when designing the oral component to give it content validity. Once this has been done, however, we can go further. We can attempt to establish the concurrent validity of the component.

To do this, we should choose at random a sample of all the students taking the test. These students would then be subjected to the full 45 minute oral component necessary for coverage of all the functions, using perhaps four scorers to ensure reliable scoring (see next chapter). This would be the criterion test against which the shorter test would be judged. The students' scores on the full test would be compared with the ones they obtained on the ten-minute session, which would have been conducted and scored in the usual way, without knowledge of their performance on the longer version. If the comparison between the two sets of scores reveals a high level of agreement, then the shorter version of the oral component may be considered valid, inasmuch as it gives results similar to those obtained with the longer version. If, on the other hand, the two sets of scores show little agreement, the shorter version cannot be considered valid; it cannot be used as a dependable measure of achievement with respect to the functions specified in the objectives. Of course, if ten minutes really is all that can be spared for each student, then the oral component may be included for the contribution that it makes to the assessment of students' overall achievement and for its backwash effect. But it cannot be regarded as an accurate measure in itself.

References to 'a high level of agreement' and 'little agreement' raise the question of how the level of agreement is measured. There are in fact standard procedures for comparing sets of scores in this way, which generate what is called a 'validity coefficient', a mathematical measure of similarity. Perfect agreement between two sets of scores will result in a validity coefficient of 1. Total lack of agreement will give a coefficient of zero. To get a feel for the meaning of a coefficient between these two extremes, read the contents of Box 1.

Box 1

To get a feel for what a coefficient means in terms of the level of agreement between two sets of scores, it is best to *square* that coefficient. Let us imagine that a coefficient of 0.7 is calculated between the two oral tests referred to in the main text. Squared, this becomes 0.49. If this is regarded as a proportion of one, and converted to a percentage, we get 49 per cent. On the basis of this, we can say that the scores on the short test predict 49 per cent of the variation in scores on the longer test. In broad terms, there is almost 50 per cent agreement between one set of scores and the other. A coefficient of 0.5 would signify 25 per cent agreement; a coefficient of 0.8 would indicate 64 per cent agreement. It is important to note that a 'level of agreement' of, say, 50 per cent does not mean that 50 per cent of the students would each have equivalent scores on the two versions. We are dealing with an overall measure of agreement that does not refer to the individual scores of students. This explanation of how to interpret validity coefficients is very brief and necessarily rather crude. For a better understanding, the reader is referred to Appendix 1.

Whether or not a particular level of agreement is regarded as satisfactory will depend upon the purpose of the test and the importance of the decisions that are made on the basis of it. If, for example, a test of oral ability was to be used as part of the selection procedure for a high level diplomatic post, then a coefficient of 0.7 might well be regarded as too low for a shorter test to be substituted for a full and thorough test of oral ability. The saving in time would not be worth the risk of appointing someone with insufficient ability in the relevant foreign language. On the other hand, a coefficient of the same size might be perfectly acceptable for a brief interview forming part of a placement test.

It should be said that the criterion for concurrent validation is not necessarily a proven, longer test. A test may be validated against, for example, teachers' assessments of their students, provided that the assessments themselves can be relied on. This would be appropriate where a test was developed which claimed to be measuring something different from all existing tests, as was said of at least one quite recently developed 'communicative' test.

The second kind of criterion-related validity is *predictive validity*. This concerns the degree to which a test can predict candidates' *future* performance. An example would be how well a proficiency test could predict a student's ability to cope with a graduate course at a British university. The criterion measure here might be an assessment of the student's English as perceived by his or her supervisor at the university, or it could be the outcome of the course (pass/fail etc.). The choice of criterion measure raises interesting issues. Should we rely on the subjective and untrained judgements of supervisors? How helpful is it to use final outcome as the criterion measure when so many factors other than ability in English (such as subject knowledge, intelligence, motivation, health and happiness) will have contributed to every outcome? Where outcome is used as the criterion measure, a validity coefficient of around 0.4 (only 20 per cent agreement) is about as high as one can expect. This is partly because of the other factors, and partly because those students whose English the test predicted would be inadequate are not normally permitted to take the course, and so the test's (possible) accuracy in predicting problems for those students goes unrecognised. As a result, a validity coefficient of this order is generally regarded as satisfactory. The further reading section at the end of the chapter gives references to the recent reports on the validation of the British Council's ELTS test, in which these issues are discussed at length.

Another example of predictive validity would be where an attempt was made to validate a placement test. Placement tests attempt to predict the most appropriate class for any particular student. Validation would involve an enquiry, once courses were under way, into the proportion of students who were thought to be misplaced. It would then be a matter of comparing the number of misplacements (and their effect on teaching and learning) with the cost of developing and administering a test which would place students more accurately.

Construct validity

A test, part of a test, or a testing technique is said to have construct validity if it can be demonstrated that it measures just the ability which it is supposed to measure. The word 'construct' refers to any underlying ability (or trait) which is hypothesised in a theory of language ability. One might hypothesise, for example, that the ability to read involves a number of sub-abilities, such as the ability to guess the meaning of unknown words from the context in which they are met. It would be a matter of empirical research to establish whether or not such a distinct ability existed and could be measured. If we attempted to measure that ability in a particular test, then that part of the test would have construct validity only if we were able to demonstrate that we were indeed measuring just that ability.

Gross, commonsense constructs like 'reading ability' and 'writing ability' are, in my view, unproblematical. Similarly, the direct measurement of writing ability, for instance, should not cause us too much concern: even without research we can be fairly confident that we are measuring a distinct and meaningful ability. Once we try to measure such an ability indirectly, however, we can no longer take for granted what we are doing. We need to look to a theory of writing ability for guidance as to the form an indirect test should take, its content and techniques.

Let us imagine that we are indeed planning to construct an indirect test of writing ability which must for reasons of practicality be multiple choice. Our theory of writing tells us that underlying writing ability are a number of sub-abilities, such as control of punctuation, sensitivity to demands on style, and so on. We construct items that are meant to measure these sub-abilities and administer them as a pilot test. How do we know that this test really is measuring writing ability? One step we would almost certainly take is to obtain extensive samples of the writing ability of the group to whom the test is first administered, and have these reliably scored. We would then compare scores on the pilot test with the scores given for the samples of writing. If there is a high level of agreement (and a coefficient of the kind described in the previous section can be calculated), then we have evidence that we are measuring writing ability with the test.

So far, however, though we may have developed a satisfactory indirect test of writing, we have not demonstrated the reality of the underlying constructs (control of punctuation etc.). To do this we might administer a series of specially constructed tests, measuring each of the constructs by a number of different methods. In addition, compositions written by the people who took the tests could be scored separately for performance in relation to the hypothesised constructs (control of punctuation, for example). In this way, for each person, we would obtain a set of scores for each of the constructs. Coefficients could then be calculated between the various measures. If the coefficients between scores on the same construct are consistently higher than those between scores on different constructs, then we have evidence that we are indeed measuring separate and identifiable constructs.

Construct validation is a research activity, the means by which theories are put to the test and are confirmed, modified, or abandoned. It is through construct validation that language testing can be put on a sounder, more scientific footing. But it will not all happen overnight; there is a long way to go. In the meantime, the practical language tester should try to keep abreast of what *is* known. When in doubt, where it is possible, direct testing of abilities is recommended.

Face validity

A test is said to have face validity if it *looks* as if it measures what it is supposed to measure. For example, a test which pretended to measure pronunciation ability but which did not require the candidate to speak (and there have been some) might be thought to lack face validity. This would be true even if the test's construct and criterion-related validity could be demonstrated. Face validity is hardly a scientific concept, yet it is very important. A test which does not have face validity may not be accepted by candidates, teachers, education authorities or employers. It may simply not be used; and if it is used, the candidates' reaction to it may mean that they do not perform on it in a way that truly reflects their ability. Novel techniques, particularly those which provide indirect measures, have to be introduced slowly, with care, and with convincing explanations.

The use of validity

What use is the reader to make of the notion of validity? First, every effort should be made in constructing tests to ensure content validity. Where possible, the tests should be validated empirically against some criterion. Particularly where it is intended to use indirect testing, reference should be made to the research literature to confirm that measurement of the relevant underlying constructs has been demonstrated using the testing techniques that are to be used (this may often result in disappointment – another reason for favouring direct testing!).

Any published test should supply details of its validation, without which its validity (and suitability) can hardly be judged by a potential purchaser. Tests for which validity information is not available should be treated with caution.

READER ACTIVITIES

Consider any tests with which you are familiar. Assess each of them in terms of the various kinds of validity that have been presented in this chapter. What empirical evidence is there that the test is valid? If evidence is lacking, how would you set about gathering it?

Further reading

For general discussion of test validity and ways of measuring it, see Anastasi (1976). For an interesting recent example of test validation (of the British Council ELTS test) in which a number of important issues are raised, see Criper and Davies (1988) and Hughes, Porter and Weir (1988). For the argument (with which I do not agree) that there is no criterion against which 'communicative' language tests can be validated (in the sense of criterion-related validity), see Morrow (1986). Bachman and Palmer (1981) is a good example of construct validation. For a collection of papers on language testing research, see Oller (1983).

5 Reliability

Imagine that a hundred students take a 100-item test at three o'clock one Thursday afternoon. The test is not impossibly difficult or ridiculously easy for these students, so they do not all get zero or a perfect score of 100. Now what if in fact they had not taken the test on the Thursday but had taken it at three o'clock the previous afternoon? Would we expect each student to have got exactly the same score on the Wednesday as they actually did on the Thursday? The answer to this question must be *no*. Even if we assume that the test is excellent, that the conditions of administration are almost identical, that the scoring calls for no judgement on the part of the scorers and is carried out with perfect care, and that no learning or forgetting has taken place during the one-day interval – nevertheless we would not expect every individual to get precisely the same score on the Wednesday as they got on the Thursday. Human beings are not like that; they simply do not behave in exactly the same way on every occasion, even when the circumstances seem identical.

But if this is the case, it would seem to imply that we can never have complete trust in any set of test scores. We know that the scores would have been different if the test had been administered on the previous or the following day. This is inevitable, and we must accept it. What we have to do is construct, administer and score tests in such a way that the scores actually obtained on a test on a particular occasion are likely to be *very similar* to those which would have been obtained if it had been administered to the same students with the same ability, but at a different time. The more similar the scores would have been, the more *reliable* the test is said to be.

Look at the hypothetical data in Table 1a). They represent the scores obtained by ten students who took a 100-item test (A) on a particular occasion, and those that they would have obtained if they had taken it a day later. Compare the two sets of scores. (Do not worry for the moment about the fact that we would never be able to obtain this information. Ways of estimating what scores people would have got on another occasion are discussed later. The most obvious of these is simply to have people take the same test twice.) Note the size of the difference between the two scores for each student.

TABLE 1a) SCORES ON TEST A (INVENTED DATA)

Student	Score obtained	Score which would have been obtained on the following day
Bill	68	82
Mary	46	28
Ann	19	34
Harry	89	67
Cyril	43	63
Pauline	56	59
Don	43	35
Colin	27	23
Irene	76	62
Sue	62	49

Now look at Table 1b), which displays the same kind of information for a second 100-item test (B). Again note the difference in scores for each student.

TABLE 1b) SCORES ON TEST B (INVENTED DATA)

Student	Score obtained	Score which would have been obtained on the following day
Bill	65	69
Mary	48	52
Ann	23	21
Harry	85	90
Cyril	44	39
Pauline	56	59
Don	38	35
Colin	19	16
Irene	67	62
Sue	52	57

Which test seems the more reliable? The differences between the two sets of scores are much smaller for Test B than for Test A. On the evidence that we have here (and in practice we would not wish to make claims about reliability on the basis of such a small number of individuals), Test B appears to be more reliable than Test A.

Look now at Table 1c), which represents scores of the same students on an interview using a *five-point scale*.

TABLE 1c) SCORES ON INTERVIEW (INVENTED DATA)

Student	Score obtained	Score which would have been obtained on the following day
Bill	5	3
Mary	4	5
Ann	2	4
Harry	5	2
Cyril	2	4
Pauline	3	5
Don	3	1
Colin	1	2
Irene	4	5
Sue	3	1

In one sense the two sets of interview scores are very similar. The largest difference between a student's actual score and the one which would have been obtained on the following day is 3. But the largest *possible* difference is only 4! Really the two sets of scores are very different. This becomes apparent once we compare the size of the differences *between* students with the size of differences between scores for individual students. They are of about the same order of magnitude. The result of this can be seen if we place the students in order according to their interview score, the highest first. The order based on their actual scores is markedly different from the one based on the scores they would have obtained if they had had the interview on the following day. This interview turns out in fact not to be very reliable at all.

The reliability coefficient

It is possible to quantify the reliability of a test in the form of a *reliability coefficient*. Reliability coefficients are like validity coefficients (Chapter 4). They allow us to compare the reliability of different tests. The ideal reliability coefficient is 1 – a test with a reliability coefficient of 1 is one which would give precisely the same results for a particular set of candidates regardless of when it happened to be administered. A test which had a reliability coefficient of zero (and let us hope that no such test exists!) would give sets of results quite unconnected with each other, in the sense that the score that someone actually got on a Wednesday would be no help at all in attempting to predict the score he or she would get if they took the test the day after. It is between the two extremes of 1 and zero that genuine test reliability coefficients are to be found.

Certain authors have suggested how high a reliability coefficient we should expect for different types of language tests. Lado (1961), for example, says that good vocabulary, structure and reading tests are usually in the .90 to .99 range, while auditory comprehension tests are more often in the .80 to .89 range. Oral production tests may be in the .70 to .79 range. He adds that a reliability coefficient of .85 might be considered high for an oral production test but low for a reading test. These suggestions reflect what Lado sees as the difficulty in achieving reliability in the testing of the different abilities. In fact the reliability coefficient that is to be sought will depend also on other considerations, most particularly the importance of the decisions that are to be taken on the basis of the test. The more important the decisions, the greater reliability we must demand: if we are to refuse someone the opportunity to study overseas because of their score on a language test, then we have to be pretty sure that their score would not have been much different if they had taken the test a day or two earlier or later. The next section will explain how the reliability coefficient can be used to arrive at another figure (the standard error of measurement) to estimate likely differences of this kind. Before this is done, however, something has to be said about the way in which reliability coefficients are arrived at.

The first requirement is to have two sets of scores for comparison. The most obvious way of obtaining these is to get a group of subjects to take the same test twice. This is known as the *test-retest* method. The drawbacks are not difficult to see. If the second administration of the test is too soon after the first, then subjects are likely to recall items and their responses to them, making the same responses more likely and the reliability spuriously high. If there is too long a gap between administrations, then learning (or forgetting!) will have taken place, and the coefficient will be lower than it should be. However long the gap, the subjects are unlikely to be very motivated to take the same test twice, and this too is likely to have a depressing effect on the coefficient. These effects are reduced somewhat by the use of two different forms of the same test (the *alternate forms* method). However, alternate forms are often simply not available.

It turns out, surprisingly, that the most common methods of obtaining the necessary two sets of scores involve only *one* administration of *one* test. Such methods provide us with a coefficient of 'internal consistency'. The most basic of these is the *split half* method. In this the subjects take the test in the usual way, but each subject is given *two* scores. One score is for one half of the test, the second score is for the other half. The two sets of scores are then used to obtain the reliability coefficient as if the whole test had been taken twice. In order for this method to work, it is necessary for the test to be split into two halves which are really equivalent, through the careful matching of items (in fact where items in the test have been ordered in terms of difficulty, a split into odd-numbered items and even-numbered items may be adequate). It can be seen that this method is rather like the alternate forms method, except that the two 'forms' are only half the length.[1]

It has been demonstrated empirically that this altogether more economical method will indeed give good estimates of alternate forms coefficients, provided that the alternate forms are closely equivalent to each other. Details of other methods of estimating reliability and of carrying out the necessary statistical calculations are to be found in Appendix 1.

The standard error of measurement and the true score

While the reliability coefficient allows us to compare the reliability of tests, it does not tell us directly how close an individual's actual score is to what he or she might have scored on another occasion. With a little further calculation, however, it is possible to estimate how close a person's actual score is to what is called their 'true score'.

Imagine that it were possible for someone to take the same language test over and over again, an indefinitely large number of times, without their performance being affected by having already taken the test, and without their ability in the language changing. Unless the test is perfectly reliable, and provided that it is not so easy or difficult that the student always gets full marks or zero, we would expect their scores on the various administrations to vary. If we had all of these scores we would be able to calculate their average score, and it would seem not unreasonable to think of this average as the one that best represents the student's ability with respect to this particular test. It is this score, which for obvious reasons we can never know for certain, which is referred to as the candidate's *true score*.

We are able to make statements about the probability that a candidate's true score (the one which best represents their ability on the test) is within a certain number of points of the score they actually obtained on the test. In order to do this, we first have to calculate *the standard error of measurement* of the particular test. The calculation (described in

1. Because of the reduced length, which will cause the coefficient to be less than it would be for the whole test, a statistical adjustment has to be made (see Appendix 1 for details).

Appendix 1) is very straightforward, and is based on the reliability coefficient and a measure of the spread of all the scores on the test (for a given spread of scores the greater the reliability coefficient, the smaller will be the standard error of measurement). How such statements can be made using the standard error of measurement of the test is best illustrated by an example.

Suppose that a test has a standard error of measurement of 5. An individual scores 56 on that test. We are then in a position to make the following statements:[2]

We can be about 68 per cent certain that the person's true score lies in the range of 51 to 61 (i.e. within one standard error of measurement of the score actually obtained on this occasion).

We can be about 95 per cent certain that their true score is in the range 46 to 66 (i.e. within two standard errors of measurement of the score actually obtained).

We can be 99.7 per cent certain that their true score is in the range 41 to 71 (i.e. within three standard errors of measurement of the score actually obtained).

These statements are based on what is known about the pattern of scores that would occur if it were in fact possible for someone to take the test repeatedly in the way described above. About 68 per cent of their scores would be within one standard error of measurement, and so on. If in fact they only take the test once, we cannot be sure how their score on that occasion relates to their true score, but we are still able to make probabilistic statements as above.[3]

In the end, the statistical rationale is not important. What *is* important is to recognise how we can use the standard error of measurement to inform decisions that we take on the basis of test scores. We should, for example, be very wary of taking important negative decisions about people's future if the standard error of measurement indicates that their

2. These statistical statements are based on what is known about the way a person's scores would tend to be distributed if they took the same test an indefinitely large number of times (without the experience of any test-taking occasion affecting performance on any other occasion). The scores would follow what is called a normal distribution (see Woods, Fletcher, and Hughes, 1986, for discussion beyond the scope of the present book). It is the known structure of the normal distribution which allows us to say what percentage of scores will fall within a certain range (for example about 68 per cent of scores will fall within one standard error of measurement of the true score). Since about 68 per cent of actual scores will be within one standard error of measurement of the true score, we can be about 68 per cent certain that any particular actual score will be within one standard error of measurement of the true score.

3. It should be clear that there is no such thing as a 'good' or a 'bad' standard error of measurement. It is the particular use made of particular scores in relation to a particular standard error of measurement which may be considered acceptable or unacceptable.

true score is quite likely to be equal to or above the score that would lead to a positive decision, even though their actual score is below it. For this reason, all published tests should provide users with not only the reliability coefficient but also the standard error of measurement.

We have seen the importance of reliability. If a test is not reliable then we know that the actual scores of many individuals are likely to be quite different from their true scores. This means that we can place little reliance on those scores. Even where reliability is quite high, the standard error of measurement serves to remind us that in the case of *some* individuals there is quite possibly a large discrepancy between actual score and true score. This should make us very cautious about making important decisions on the basis of the test scores of candidates whose actual scores place them close to the cut-off point (the point that divides 'passes' from 'fails'). We should at least consider the possibility of gathering further relevant information on the language ability of such candidates.

Having seen the importance of reliability, we shall consider, later in the chapter, how to make our tests more reliable. Before that, however, we shall look at another aspect of reliability.

Scorer reliability

In the first example given in this chapter we spoke about scores on a multiple choice test. It was most unlikely, we thought, that every candidate would get precisely the same score on both of two possible administrations of the test. We assumed, however, that scoring of the test would be 'perfect'. That is, if a particular candidate did perform in exactly the same way on the two occasions, they would be given the same score on both occasions. That is, any one scorer would give the same score on the two occasions, and this would be the same score as would be given by any other scorer on either occasion. It is possible to quantify the level of agreement given by different scorers on different occasions by means of a scorer reliability coefficient which can be interpreted in a similar way as the test reliability coefficient. In the case of the multiple choice test just described the scorer reliability coefficient would be 1. As we noted in Chapter 3, when scoring requires no judgement, and could in principle or in practice be carried out by a computer, the test is said to be objective. Only carelessness should cause the reliability coefficients of objective tests to fall below 1.

However, we did not assume perfectly consistent scoring in the case of the interview scores discussed earlier in the chapter. It would probably have seemed to the reader an unreasonable assumption. We can accept that scorers should be able to be consistent when there is only one easily recognised correct response. But when a degree of judgement is called for on the part of the scorer, as in the scoring of performance in an interview, perfect consistency is not to be expected. Such subjective tests will not have reliability coefficients of 1! Indeed there was a time when many people thought that scorer reliability coefficients (and also the reliability of the test) would always be too low to justify the use of subjective measures of language ability in serious language testing. This view is less widely held today. While the perfect reliability of objective tests is not obtainable in subjective tests, there are ways of making it sufficiently high for test results to be valuable. It is possible, for instance, to obtain scorer reliability coefficients of over 0.9 for the scoring of compositions.

It is perhaps worth making explicit something about the relationship between scorer reliability and test reliability. If the scoring of a test is not reliable, then the test results cannot be reliable either. Indeed the test reliability coefficient will almost certainly be *lower than* scorer reliability, since other sources of unreliability will be additional to what enters through imperfect scoring. In a case I know of, the scorer reliability coefficient on a composition writing test was .92, while the reliability coefficient for the test was .84. Variability in the performance of individual candidates accounted for the difference between the two coefficients.

How to make tests more reliable

As we have seen, there are two components of test reliability: the performance of candidates from occasion to occasion, and the reliability of the scoring. We will begin by suggesting ways of achieving consistent performances from candidates and then turn our attention to scorer reliability.

Take enough samples of behaviour

Other things being equal, the more items that you have on a test, the more reliable that test will be. This seems intuitively right. If we wanted to know how good an archer someone was, we wouldn't rely on the evidence of a single shot at the target. That one shot could be quite unrepresentative of their ability. To be satisfied that we had a really reliable measure of the ability we would want to see a large number of shots at the target.

The same is true for language testing. It has been demonstrated empirically that the addition of further items will make a test more reliable. There is even a formula (the Spearman-Brown formula, see the Appendix) that allows one to estimate how many extra items similar to the ones already in the test will be needed to increase the reliability coefficient to a required level. One thing to bear in mind, however, is that the additional items should be independent of each other and of existing items. Imagine a reading test that asks the question: 'Where did the thief hide the jewels?' If an additional item following that took the form 'What was unusual about the hiding place?', it would not make a full contribution to an increase in the reliability of the test. Why not? Because it is hardly possible for someone who got the original question wrong to get the supplementary question right. Such candidates are effectively prevented from answering the additional question; for them, in reality, there is no additional question. We do not get an additional sample of their behaviour, so the reliability of our estimate of their ability is not increased.

Each additional item should as far as possible represent a fresh start for the candidate. By doing this we are able to gain additional information on all of the candidates, information which will make test results more reliable. The use of the word 'item' should not be taken to mean only brief questions and answers. In a test of writing, for example, where candidates have to produce a number of passages, each of those passages is to be regarded as an item. The more independent passages there are, the more reliable will be the test. In the same way, in an interview used to test oral ability, the candidate should be given as many 'fresh starts' as possible. More detailed implications of the need to obtain sufficiently large samples of behaviour will be outlined later in the book, in chapters devoted to the testing of particular abilities.

While it is important to make a test long enough to achieve satisfactory reliability, it should not be made so long that the candidates become so bored or tired that the behaviour that they exhibit becomes unrepresentative of their ability. At the same time, it may often be necessary to resist pressure to make a test shorter than is appropriate. The usual argument for shortening a test is that it is not practical. The answer to this is that accurate information does not come cheaply: if such information is needed, then the price has to be paid. In general, the more important the decisions based on a test, the longer the test should be. Jephthah used the pronunciation of the word 'shibboleth' as a test to distinguish his own men from Ephraimites, who could not pronounce *sh*. Those who failed the test were executed. Any of Jephthah's own men killed in error might have wished for a longer, more reliable test.

Do not allow candidates too much freedom

In some kinds of language test there is a tendency to offer candidates a choice of questions and then to allow them a great deal of freedom in the way that they answer the ones that they have chosen. An example would be a test of writing where the candidates are simply given a selection of titles from which to choose. Such a procedure is likely to have a depressing effect on the reliability of the test. The more freedom that is given, the greater is likely to be the difference between the performance actually elicited and the performance that would have been elicited had the test been taken, say, a day later. In general, therefore, candidates should not be given a choice, and the range over which possible answers might vary should be restricted. Compare the following writing tasks:

a) Write a composition on tourism.
b) Write a composition on tourism in this country.
c) Write a composition on how we might develop the tourist industry in this country.
d) Discuss the following measures intended to increase the number of foreign tourists coming to this country:
   i)   More/better advertising and/or information (where? what form should it take?).
   ii) Improve facilities (hotels, transportation, communication etc.).
   iii) Training of personnel (guides, hotel managers etc.).

The successive tasks impose more and more control over what is written. The fourth task is likely to be a much more reliable indicator of writing ability than the first.

The general principle of restricting the freedom of candidates will be taken up again in chapters relating to particular skills. It should perhaps be said here, however, that in restricting the students we must be careful not to distort too much the task that we really want to see them perform. The potential tension between reliability and validity is taken up at the end of the chapter.

Write unambiguous items

It is essential that candidates should not be presented with items whose meaning is not clear or to which there is an acceptable answer which the test writer has not anticipated. In a reading test I once set the following open-ended question, based on a lengthy reading passage about English accents and dialects: Where does the author direct the reader who is interested in non-standard dialects of English? The expected answer was the *Further reading* section of the book, which is where the reader was directed to. A number of candidates answered 'page 3', which was the place in the text where the author actually said that the interested reader should look in the *Further reading* section. Only the alertness of those scoring the test revealed that there was a completely unanticipated correct answer to the question. If that had not happened, then a correct answer would have been scored as incorrect. The fact that an individual candidate might interpret the question in different ways on different occasions means that the item is not contributing fully to the reliability of the test.

The best way to arrive at unambiguous items is, having drafted them, to subject them to the critical scrutiny of colleagues, who should try as hard as they can to find alternative interpretations to the ones intended. If this task is entered into in the right spirit, one of good-natured perversity, most of the problems can be identified before the test is administered. Pretesting of the items on a group of people comparable to those for whom the test is intended (see Chapter 7) should reveal the remainder. Where pretesting is not practicable, scorers must be on the lookout for patterns of response that indicate that there are problem items.

Provide clear and explicit instructions

This applies both to written and oral instructions. If it is possible for candidates to misinterpret what they are asked to do, then on some occasions some of them certainly will. It is by no means always the weakest candidates who are misled by ambiguous instructions; indeed it is often the better candidate who is able to provide the alternative interpretation. A common fault of tests written for the students of a particular teaching institution is the supposition that the students all know what is intended by carelessly worded instructions. The frequency of the complaint that students are unintelligent, have been stupid, have wilfully misunderstood what they were asked to do, reveals that the supposition is often unwarranted. Test writers should not rely on the students' powers of telepathy to elicit the desired behaviour. Again, the use of colleagues to criticise drafts of instructions (including those which will be spoken) is the best means of avoiding problems. Spoken instructions should always be read from a prepared text in order to avoid introducing confusion.

Ensure that tests are well laid out and perfectly legible

Too often, institutional tests are badly typed (or handwritten), have too much text in too small a space, and are poorly reproduced. As a result, students are faced with additional tasks which are not ones meant to measure their language ability. Their variable performance on the unwanted tasks will lower the reliability of a test.

Candidates should be familiar with format and testing techniques

If any aspect of a test is unfamiliar to candidates, they are likely to perform less well than they would do otherwise (on subsequently taking a parallel version, for example). For this reason, every effort must be made to ensure that all candidates have the opportunity to learn just what will be required of them. This may mean the distribution of sample tests (or of past test papers), or at least the provision of practice materials in the case of tests set within teaching institutions.

Provide uniform and non-distracting conditions of administration

The greater the differences between one administration of a test and another, the greater the differences one can expect between a candidate's performance on the two occasions. Great care should be taken to ensure uniformity. For example, timing should be specified and strictly adhered to; the acoustic conditions should be similar for all administrations of a listening test. Every precaution should be taken to maintain a quiet setting with no distracting sounds or movements.

We turn now to ways of obtaining *scorer reliability*, which, as we saw above, is essential to test reliability.

Use items that permit scoring which is as objective as possible

This may appear to be a recommendation to use multiple choice items, which permit completely objective scoring. This is not intended. While it would be mistaken to say that multiple choice items are never appropriate, it is certainly true that there are many circumstances in which they are quite inappropriate. What is more, good multiple choice items are notoriously difficult to write and always require extensive pretesting. A substantial part of Chapter 8 is given over to a discussion of the construction and use of multiple choice items.

An alternative to multiple choice is the open-ended item which has a unique, possibly one-word, correct response which the candidates produce themselves. This too should ensure objective scoring, but in fact problems with such matters as spelling which makes a candidate's meaning unclear (say, in a listening test) often make demands on the scorer's judgement. The longer the required response, the greater the difficulties of this kind. One way of dealing with this is to structure the candidate's response by providing part of it. For example, the open-ended question *What was different about the results?* may be designed to elicit the response *Success was closely associated with high motivation.* This is likely to cause problems for scoring. Greater scorer reliability will probably be achieved if the question is followed by:

.... *was more closely associated with*........................

Items of this kind are discussed in later chapters.

Make comparisons between candidates as direct as possible

This reinforces the suggestion already made that candidates should not be given a choice of items and that they should be limited in the way that they are allowed to respond. Scoring the compositions all on one topic will be more reliable than if the candidates are allowed to choose from six topics, as has been the case in some well-known tests. The scoring should be all the more reliable if the compositions are guided as in the example above, in the section, *Do not allow candidates too much freedom.*

Provide a detailed scoring key

This should specify acceptable answers and assign points for partially correct responses. For high scorer reliability the key should be as detailed as possible in its assignment of points. It should be the outcome of efforts to anticipate all possible responses and have been subjected to group criticism. (This advice applies only where responses can be classed as partially or totally 'correct', not in the case of compositions, for instance.)

Train scorers

This is especially important where scoring is most subjective. The scoring of compositions, for example, should not be assigned to anyone who has not learned to score accurately compositions from past administrations. After each administration, patterns of scoring should be analysed. Individuals whose scoring deviates markedly and inconsistently from the norm should not be used again.

Agree acceptable responses and appropriate scores at outset of scoring

A sample of scripts should be taken immediately after the administration of the test. Where there are compositions, archetypical representatives of different levels of ability should be selected. Only when all scorers are agreed on the scores to be given to these should real scoring begin. Much more will be said in Chapter 9 about the scoring of compositions.

For short answer questions, the scorers should note any difficulties they have in assigning points (the key is unlikely to have anticipated every relevant response), and bring these to the attention of whoever is supervising that part of the scoring. Once a decision has been taken as to the points to be assigned, the supervisor should convey it to all the scorers concerned.

Identify candidates by number, not name

Scorers inevitably have expectations of candidates that they know. Except in purely objective testing, this will affect the way that they score. Studies have shown that even where the candidates are unknown to the scorers, the name on a script (or a photograph) will make a significant difference to the scores given. For example, a scorer may be influenced by the gender or nationality of a name into making predictions which can affect the score given. The identification of candidates only by number will reduce such effects.

Employ multiple, independent scoring

As a general rule, and certainly where testing is subjective, all scripts should be scored by at least two independent scorers. Neither scorer should know how the other has scored a test paper. Scores should be recorded on separate score sheets and passed to a third, senior, colleague, who compares the two sets of scores and investigates discrepancies.

Reliability and validity

To be valid a test must provide consistently accurate measurements. It must therefore be reliable. A reliable test, however, may not be valid at all. For example, as a writing test we might require candidates to write down the translation equivalents of 500 words in their own language. This could well be a reliable test; but it is unlikely to be a valid test of writing.

In our efforts to make tests reliable, we must be wary of reducing their validity. Earlier in this chapter it was admitted that restricting the scope of what candidates are permitted to write in a composition might diminish the validity of the task. This depends in part on what exactly we are trying to measure by setting the task. If we are interested in candidates' ability to structure a composition, then it would be hard to justify providing them with a structure in order to increase reliability. At the same time we would still try to restrict candidates in ways which would not render their performance on the task invalid.

There will always be some tension between reliability and validity. The tester has to balance gains in one against losses in the other.

READER ACTIVITIES

1. What published tests are you familiar with? Try to find out their reliability coefficients. (Check the manual; check to see if there is a review in Alderson *et al.* 1987.) What method was used to arrive at these? What are the standard errors of measurement?
2. The TOEFL test has a standard error of measurement of 15. A particular American college states that it requires a score of 600 on the test for entry. What would you think of students applying to that college and making scores of 605, 600, 595, 590, 575?
3. Look at your own institutional tests. Using the list of points in the chapter, say in what ways you could improve their reliability.
4. What examples can you think of where there would be a tension between reliability and validity? In cases that you know, do you think the right balance has been struck?

Further reading

For more on reliability in general, see Anastasi (1976). For the more mathematically minded, Krzanowski and Woods' (1984) article on reliability will be of interest (note that errata in that article appear in a later issue – 1.2, 1984 – of the journal *Language Testing*). For what I think is an exaggerated view of the difficulty of achieving high reliability in more communicative tasks, see Lado (1961).

6 Achieving beneficial backwash

In the first chapter of this book it was claimed that testing could, and should, have a beneficial backwash effect on teaching and learning. This chapter attempts to say how such an effect can be achieved.

Test the abilities whose development you want to encourage

For example, if you want to encourage oral ability, then test oral ability. This is very obvious, a straightforward matter of content validity, yet it is surprising how often it is not done. There is a tendency to test what it is easiest to test rather than what it is most important to test. Reasons advanced for not testing particular abilities may take many forms. It is often said, for instance, that sufficiently high reliability cannot be obtained when a form of testing (such as an oral interview) requires subjective scoring. This is simply not the case, and in addition to the advice already given in the previous chapter, more detailed suggestions for achieving satisfactory reliability of subjective tests are to be found in Chapters 9 and 10. The other most frequent reason given for not testing is the expense involved in terms of time and money. This is discussed later in the chapter.

It is important not only that certain abilities should be tested, but also that they should be given sufficient weight in relation to other abilities. I well remember my French master telling the class that, since the oral component of the General Certificate of Education examination in French (which we were to take later in the year) carried so few marks, we should not waste our time preparing for it. The examining board concerned was hardly encouraging beneficial backwash.

Sample widely and unpredictably

Normally a test can measure only a sample of everything included in the specifications. It is important that the sample taken should represent as far as possible the full scope of what is specified. If not, if the sample is taken from a restricted area of the specifications, then the backwash effect will tend to be felt only in that area. The new TOEFL writing test (referred to in Chapter 1) will set only two kinds of task: compare/contrast; describe/interpret chart or graph. The likely outcome is that much preparation for the test will be limited to those two types of task. The backwash effect may not be as beneficial as it might have been had a wider range of tasks been used.

Whenever the content of a test becomes highly predictable, teaching and learning are likely to concentrate on what can be predicted. An effort should therefore be made to test across the full range of the specifications (in the case of achievement tests, this should be equivalent to a fully elaborated set of objectives), even where this involves elements that lend themselves less readily to testing.

Use direct testing

As we saw in Chapter 3, direct testing implies the testing of performance skills, with texts and tasks as authentic as possible. If we test directly the skills that we are interested in fostering, then practice for the test represents practice in those skills. If we want people to learn to write compositions, we should get them to write compositions in the test. If a course objective is that students should be able to read scientific articles, then we should get them to do *that* in the test. Immediately we begin to test indirectly, we are removing an incentive for students to practise in the way that we want them to.

Make testing criterion-referenced

If test specifications make clear just what candidates have to be able to do, and with what degree of success, then students will have a clear picture of what they have to achieve. What is more, they know that if they do perform the tasks at the criterial level, then they will be successful on the test, regardless of how other students perform. Both these things will help to motivate students. Where testing is not criterion-referenced, it becomes easy for teachers and students to assume that a certain (perhaps very high) percentage of candidates will pass, almost regardless of the absolute standard that they reach.

The possibility exists of having a series of criterion-referenced tests, each representing a different level of achievement or proficiency. The tests are constructed such that a 'pass' is obtained only by completing the great majority of the test tasks successfully. Students take only the test (or tests) on which they are expected to be successful. As a result, they are spared the dispiriting, demotivating experience of taking a test on which they can, for example, respond correctly to fewer than half of the items (and yet be given a pass). This type of testing, I believe, should encourage positive attitudes to language learning. It is the basis of some of the new GCSE (General Certificate of Secondary Education) examinations in Britain.

Base achievement tests on objectives

If achievement tests are based on objectives, rather than on detailed teaching and textbook content, they will provide a truer picture of what has actually been achieved. Teaching and learning will tend to be evaluated against those objectives. As a result, there will be constant pressure to achieve them. This was argued more fully in Chapter 3.

Ensure test is known and understood by students and teachers

However good the *potential* backwash effect of a test may be, the effect will not be fully realised if students and those responsible for teaching do not know and understand what the test demands of them. The rationale for the test, its specifications, and sample items should be made available to everyone concerned with preparation for the test. This is particularly important when a new test is being introduced, especially if it incorporates novel testing methods. Another, equally important, reason for supplying information of this kind is to increase test reliability, as was noted in the previous chapter.

Where necessary, provide assistance to teachers

The introduction of a new test may make demands on teachers to which they are not equal. If, for example, a longstanding national test of grammatical structure and vocabulary is to be replaced by a direct test of a much more communicative nature, it is possible that many teachers will feel that they do not know how to teach communicative skills. One important reason for introducing the new test may have been to encourage communicative language teaching, but if the teachers need guidance and possibly training, and these are not given, the test will not achieve its intended effect. It may simply cause chaos and disaffection. Where new tests are meant to help change teaching, support has to be given to help effect the change.

Counting the cost

One of the desirable qualities of tests which trips quite readily off the tongue of many testers, after validity and reliability, is that of *practicality*. Other things being equal, it is good that a test should be easy and cheap to construct, administer, score and interpret. We should not forget that testing costs time and money that could be put to alternative uses.

It is unlikely to have escaped the reader's notice that at least some of the recommendations listed above for creating beneficial backwash involve more than minimal expense. The individual direct testing of some abilities will take a great deal of time, as will the reliable scoring of performance on any subjective test. The production and distribution of sample tests and the training of teachers will also be costly. It might be argued, therefore, that such procedures are impractical.

In my opinion, this would reveal an incomplete understanding of what is involved. Before we decide that we cannot afford to test in a way that will promote beneficial backwash, we have to ask ourselves a question: what will be the cost of *not* achieving beneficial backwash? When we compare the cost of the test with the waste of effort and time on the part of teachers and students in activities quite inappropriate to their true learning goals (and in some circumstances, with the potential loss to the national economy of not having more people competent in foreign languages), we are likely to decide that we cannot afford *not* to introduce a test with a powerful beneficial backwash effect.

READER ACTIVITIES

1. How would you improve the backwash effect of tests that you know? Be as specific as possible. (This is a follow-up to Activity 1 at the end of Chapter 1.)
2. Rehearse the arguments you would use to convince a sceptic that it would be worthwhile making the changes that you recommend.

Further reading

Any of the English or Welsh Examining Groups will provide, at a small cost, syllabuses and specimen papers for the new GCSE examinations in foreign languages. These illustrate some of the principles enumerated in the chapter.

7   Stages of test construction

This chapter begins by briefly laying down a set of general procedures for test construction. These are then illustrated by two examples: an achievement test and a placement test. Finally there is a short section on validation.

Statement of the problem

It cannot be said too many times that the essential first step in testing is to make oneself perfectly clear about what it is one wants to know and for what purpose. The following questions, the significance of which should be clear from previous chapters, have to be answered:

- What kind of test is it to be? Achievement (final or progress), proficiency, diagnostic, or placement?
- What is its precise purpose?
- What abilities are to be tested?
- How detailed must the results be?
- How accurate must the results be?
- How important is backwash?
- What constraints are set by unavailability of expertise, facilities, time (for construction, administration and scoring)?

Providing a solution to the problem

Once the problem is clear, then steps can be taken to solve it. It is to be hoped that a handbook of the present kind will take readers a long way towards appropriate solutions. In addition, however, efforts should be made to gather information on tests that have been designed for similar situations. If possible, samples of such tests should be obtained. There is nothing shameful in doing this; it is what professional testing bodies do when they are planning a test of a kind for which they do not already have first-hand experience. Nor does it contradict the claim made earlier that each testing situation is unique. It is not intended that other tests should simply be copied; rather that their development can serve to suggest possibilities and to help avoid the need to 'reinvent the wheel'.

Writing specifications for the test

The first form that the solution takes is a set of specifications for the test. This will include information on: content, format and timing, criterial levels of performance, and scoring procedures.

CONTENT

This refers not to the content of a single, particular version of a test, but to the entire *potential* content of any number of versions. Samples of this content will appear in individual versions of the test.

The fuller the information on content, the less arbitrary should be the subsequent decisions as to what to include in the writing of any version of the test. There is a danger, however, that in the desire to be highly specific, we may go beyond our current understanding of what the components of language ability are and what their relationship is to each other. For instance, while we may believe that many subskills contribute to the ability to read lengthy prose passages with full understanding, it seems hardly possible in our present state of knowledge to name them all or to assess their individual contributions to the more general ability. We cannot be sure that the sum of the parts that we test will amount to the whole in which we are generally most directly interested. At the same time, however, teaching practice often assumes some such knowledge, with one subskill being taught at a time. It seems to me that the safest procedure is to include in the content specifications only those elements whose contribution is fairly well established.

The way in which content is described will vary with its nature. The content of a grammar test, for example, may simply list all the relevant structures. The content of a test of a language skill, on the other hand, may be specified along a number of dimensions. The following provides a possible framework for doing this. It is not meant to be prescriptive; readers may wish to describe test content differently. The important thing is that content should be as fully specified as possible.

Operations (the tasks that candidates have to be able to carry out). For a reading test these might include, for example: scan text to locate specific information; guess meaning of unknown words from context.

Types of text For a writing test these might include: letters, forms, academic essays up to three pages in length.

Addressees This refers to the kinds of people that the candidate is expected to be able to write or speak to (for example native speakers of the same age and status); or the people for whom reading and listening materials are primarily intended (for example native-speaker university students).

Topics Topics are selected according to suitability for the candidate and the type of test.

FORMAT AND TIMING

This should specify test structure (including time allocated to components) and item types/elicitation procedures, with examples. It should state what weighting is to be assigned to each component. It should also say how many passages will normally be presented (in the case of reading or listening) or required (in the case of writing), how many items there will be in each component.

CRITERIAL LEVELS OF PERFORMANCE

The required level(s) of performance for (different levels of) success should be specified. This may involve a simple statement to the effect that, to demonstrate 'mastery', 80 per cent of the items must be responded to correctly. It may be more complex: the Basic level oral interaction specifications of the Royal Society of Arts (RSA) Test of the Communicative Use of English as a Foreign Language will serve as an example. These refer to accuracy, appropriacy, range, flexibility, and size. Thus:

	BASIC
Accuracy	Pronunciation may be heavily influenced by L1 and accented though generally intelligible. Any confusion caused by grammatical/lexical errors can be clarified by the candidate.
Appropriacy	Use of language broadly appropriate to function, though no subtlety should be expected. The intention of the speaker can be perceived without excessive effort.
Range	Severely limited range of expression is acceptable. May often have to search for a way to convey the desired meaning.

Flexibility	Need not usually take the intiative in conversation. May take time to respond to a change of topic. Interlocutor may have to make considerable allowances and often adopt a supportive role.
Size	Contributions generally limited to one or two simple utterances are acceptable.

SCORING PROCEDURES

These are most relevant where scoring will be subjective. The test constructors should be clear as to how they will achieve high scorer reliability.

Writing the test

SAMPLING

It is most unlikely that everything found under the heading of 'Content' in the specifications can be included in any one version of the test. Choices have to be made. For content validity and for beneficial backwash, the important thing is to choose widely from the whole area of content. One should not concentrate on those elements known to be easy to test. Succeeding versions of the test should also sample widely and unpredictably.

ITEM WRITING AND MODERATION

The writing of successful items (in the broadest sense, including, for example, the setting of writing tasks) is extremely difficult. No one can expect to be able consistently to produce perfect items. Some items will have to be rejected, others reworked. The best way to identify items that have to be improved or abandoned is through teamwork. Colleagues must really try to find fault; and despite the seemingly inevitable emotional attachment that item writers develop to items that they have created, they must be open to, and ready to accept, the criticisms that are offered to them. Good personal relations are a desirable quality in any test writing team.

Critical questions that may be asked include:

Is the task perfectly clear?
Is there more than one possible correct response?

Can candidates show the desired behaviour (or arrive at the correct response) without having the skill supposedly being tested?
Do candidates have enough time to perform the task(s)?

In addition to moderation, as this process is called, an attempt should be made to administer the test to native speakers of a similar educational background to future test candidates. These native speakers should score 100 per cent, or close to it. Items that prove difficult for comparable native speakers almost certainly need revision or replacement.

WRITING AND MODERATION OF SCORING KEY

Once the items have been agreed, the next task is to write the scoring key where this is appropriate. Where there is intended to be only one correct response, this is a perfectly straightforward matter. Where there are alternative acceptable responses, which may be awarded different scores, or where partial credit may be given for incomplete responses, greater care is necessary. Once again, the criticism of colleagues should be sought as a matter of course.

Pretesting

Even after careful moderation, there are likely to be some problems with every test. It is obviously better if these problems can be identified before the test is administered to the group for which it is intended. The aim should be to administer it first to a group as similar as possible to the one for which it is really intended. Problems in administration and scoring are noted. The reliability coefficients of the whole test and of its components are calculated, and individual items are analysed (see the Appendix for procedures).

It has to be accepted that, for a number of reasons, pretesting is often not feasible. In some situations a group for pretesting may simply not be available. In other situations, though a suitable group exists, it may be thought that the security of the test might be put at risk. It is often the case, therefore, that faults in a test are discovered only after it has been administered to the target group. Unless it is intended that no part of the test should be used again, it is worthwhile noting problems that become apparent during administration and scoring, and afterwards carrying out statistical analysis of the kind described in Appendix 1.

Example 1 An achievement test

Statement of the problem

There is a need for an achievement test to be administered at the end of a presessional course of training in the reading of academic texts in the social sciences and business studies (the students are graduates who are about to follow postgraduate courses in English-medium universities). The teaching institution concerned (as well as the sponsors of the students) wants to know just what progress is being made during the three-month course. The test must therefore obviously be sufficiently sensitive to measure gain over that relatively short period. While there is no call for diagnostic information on individuals, it would be useful to know, for groups, where the greatest difficulties remain at the end of the course, so that future courses may give more attention in these areas. Backwash is considered important; the test should encourage the practice of the reading skills that the students will need in their university studies. This is in fact intended to be only one of a battery of tests, and a maximum of two hours can be allowed for it. It will not be possible at the outset to write separate tests for different subject areas.

Specifications

CONTENT

Types of text   The texts should be academic (taken from textbooks and journal papers).

Addressees   Academics at postgraduate level and beyond.

Topics   The subject areas will have to be as 'neutral' as possible, since the students are from a variety of social science and business disciplines (economics, sociology, management etc.).

Operations   These are based on the stated objectives of the course, and include broad and underlying skills:

Broad skills:
1. Scan extensive written texts for pieces of information.
2. Construe the meaning of complex, closely argued passages.

Underlying skills:
(Those which are regarded as of particular importance for the development of the broad skills, and which are given particular attention in the course.)
3. Guessing the meaning of unfamiliar words from context.
4. Identifying referents of pronouns etc., often some distance removed in the text.

53

Stages of test construction

FORMAT AND TIMING[1]

Scanning 2 passages each *c.* 3,000 words in length.
15 short-answer items on each, the items in the order in which relevant information appears in the texts. 'Controlled' responses where appropriate.

> e.g. How does the middleman make a large profit in traditional rural industry?
> He ....
> and then ....

Time: 1 hour

Detailed reading 2 passages each *c.* 1,500 words in length.
7 short-answer questions on each, with guidance as to relevant part of text. 'Controlled' responses where appropriate.

> e.g. Cross-sectional studies have indicated that intelligence declines after the age of thirty. Part of the explanation for this may be that certain intelligence test tasks require ...., something of which we are less capable as we grow older.

5 meaning-from-context items from one of the detailed reading passages

> e.g. For each of the following, find a single word in the text with an equivalent meaning. Note: the word in the text may have an ending such as -*ing*, -*s*, etc.
> *highest point* (lines 20–35)

5 referent-identification items from one of the detailed reading passages

> e.g. What does each of the following refer to in the text? Be very precise.
> *the former* (line 43)

CRITERIAL LEVELS OF PERFORMANCE

Items are written such that anyone completing the course successfully should be able to respond correctly to all of them. Allowing for 'performance errors' on the part of candidates, a criterial level of 80 per cent is set. The number of students reaching this level will be the number who have succeeded in terms of the course's objectives.

SCORING PROCEDURES

There will be a detailed key, making scoring almost entirely objective. There will nevertheless be independent double scoring. Scorers will be trained to ignore irrelevant (for example grammatical) inaccuracy in responses.

---

1. Justification for choice of techniques is not presented here, since such matters are treated in subsequent chapters.

54

SAMPLING

Texts will be chosen from as wide a range of topics and types of writing as is compatible with the specifications. Draft items will only be written after the suitability of the texts has been agreed.

ITEM WRITING AND MODERATION

Items will be based on a consideration of what a competent non-specialist reader should be able to obtain from the texts. Considerable time will be set aside for moderation and rewriting of items.

KEY

There will be a key with details of partial credit for incomplete responses. This too will be subject to thorough moderation.

PRETESTING

Pretesting of texts and items sufficient for at least two versions will be carried out with students currently taking the course.

Example 2 A placement test

Statement of the problem

A commercial English language teaching institution needs a placement test. Its purpose will be to assign new students to classes at five levels: false beginners; lower intermediate; middle intermediate; upper intermediate; advanced. Course objectives at all levels are expressed in rather general 'communicative' terms, with no one skill being given greater attention than any other. As well as information on overall ability in the language, some indication of oral ability would be useful. Sufficient accuracy is required for there to be little need for changes of class once teaching is under way. Backwash is not a serious consideration. More than a thousand new students enrol within a matter of days. The test must be brief (not more than 45 minutes in length), quick and easy to administer, score and interpret. Formal interviews or other direct tests of oral ability are out of the question.

Specifications

CONTENT

Styles and topics of texts will reflect the kinds of written and spoken texts that are to be found in teaching materials at the various levels.
    As testing will be indirect, operations are dealt with under 'format'.

FORMAT AND TIMING

Cloze-type tests A series of five 20-item cloze-type passages presented in increasing order of difficulty, with blanks selected to represent

C

grammar items and vocabulary items, as well as to some extent testing overall comprehension.

Time: 30 minutes (Note: this seems very little time, but the more advanced students will find the early passages extremely easy, and will take very little time. It does not matter whether lower level students reach the later passages.)

(For examples of cloze-type passages, see next chapter.)

Partial dictation   A 20-item partial dictation test (part of what is heard by the candidates already being printed on the answer sheet). Stretches to be transcribed being ordered according to difficulty. Spelling to be ignored in scoring. To be administered in the language laboratory. Since no oral test is possible, this is intended to give some indication of oral ability.

Time: 10 minutes

e.g. The candidate hears:
'Particular consideration was given to the timing of the report'
and has to complete:
Particular consideration...................................timing.........................

In addition, information should be collected on previous training in English, as well as comments of the person who carries out the registration using English as far as possible (the registration procedure can be used as an informal, and not very reliable, oral test).

SAMPLING

As noted above, the texts are meant to provide a representative sample of the kinds of spoken and written English found at the various levels. Choice of texts will be agreed before deletions are made.

Scoring will be objective and may be carried out by non-teachers.

CRITERIAL LEVELS OF PERFORMANCE

These will be determined during pretesting (see below).

ITEM AND KEY WRITING (AND MODERATION)

Cloze-type tests   Once texts have been chosen, deletions are made and keys constructed. The mutilated passages are then presented to the moderating group. It is particularly important that there is only one acceptable response for most items (preferably no more than two or three on any item). Revised versions are presented to native speakers, and revised again if necessary.

Partial dictation   Stretches for dictation are identified in selected short passages, and answer sheets prepared. The draft test is then administered to the moderating group, who should all score 100 per cent. The main problem is likely to be with scoring, and the group should try to anticipate the kinds of spelling errors which students may make and which would make reliable scoring difficult. Changes can then be made, though unanticipated errors will probably occur during pretesting. The final key will have to take account of all of these, and be highly explicit about their treatment.

Pretesting

More passages and dictation items will be constructed than will finally be used. All of them will be pretested on current students at the various levels in the institution. Problems in administration and scoring will be noted.

Students' scores are noted on each of the cloze-type passages and the partial dictation. Total scores for the cloze-type passages and for the test as a whole are calculated. Each of these scores for each student is then compared with his or her level in the institution. The next step is to identify the 'cutting' scores which will most accurately divide the students up into their actual levels in the school. 'Misfits', those students who are assigned to the 'wrong' level by the test using these cutting scores, can be investigated; it may be that they would be as well off in the level in which the test has placed them.

Improvements in items are likely to suggest themselves during pretesting. There are also statistical procedures for combining scores on the various parts of the test to maximise its predictive power. Unfortunately, these must fall outside the scope of a book of this size.

Validation of the test

When we speak of validating a particular test, we are usually referring to criterion-related validity. We are looking for empirical evidence that the test will perform well against some criterion. Chapter 4 mentioned typical criteria against which tests are judged. In the case of the placement test above, the proportion of students that it assigned to inappropriate classes would be the basis for assessing its validity. The achievement test might be validated against the ratings of students by their current language teachers and by their future subject teachers soon after the beginning of their academic courses.

READER ACTIVITIES

On the basis of experience or intuition, try to write a specification for a test designed to measure the level of language proficiency of students applying to study an academic subject in the medium of a foreign language at an overseas university. Compare your specification with those of tests which actually have been constructed for that purpose. For

English, you might look at ELTS (British Council), TEEP (Test of English for Educational Purposes), and TOEFL. If specifications are not available, you will have to infer them from sample tests or past papers.

Further reading

It is useful to study existing specifications. Specifications for the UCLES/ RSA Test in the Communicative Use of English as a Foreign Language can be obtained from UCLES, 1–3 Hills Road, Cambridge. (NB This examination is currently under review. The revised version is expected to be ready from September, 1990. The first administration will not be before November, 1990.) Those for TEEP are to be found in Weir (1988a, 1988b).

8 Test techniques and testing overall ability

What are test techniques? Quite simply they are means of eliciting behaviour from candidates which will tell us about their language abilities. What we need are techniques which:

1. will elicit behaviour which is a reliable and valid indicator of the ability in which we are interested;
2. will elicit behaviour which can be reliably scored;
3. are as economical of time and effort as possible;
4. will have a beneficial backwash effect.

From Chapter 9 onwards, techniques are discussed in relation to particular abilities. This chapter discusses one technique, multiple choice, which has been recommended and used for the testing of many language abilities. It then goes on to examine the use of techniques which may be used to test 'overall ability'.

Multiple choice

Multiple choice items take many forms, but their basic structure is as follows.

There is a *stem*:

Enid has been here _____ half an hour.

and a number of *options*, one of which is correct, the others being *distractors*:

A. during
B. for
C. while
D. since

It is the candidate's task to identify the correct or most appropriate option (in this case B).

Perhaps the most obvious advantage of multiple choice, referred to earlier in the book, is that scoring can be perfectly reliable. Scoring should also be rapid and economical. A further considerable advantage is that, since in order to respond the candidate has only to make a mark on the paper, it is possible to include more items than would otherwise be possible in a given period of time. As we know from Chapter 5, this is likely to make for greater test reliability.

The advantages of the multiple choice technique were so highly regarded at one time that it almost seemed that it was the *only* way to test. While many laymen have always been sceptical of what could be achieved through multiple choice testing, it is only fairly recently that the technique's limitations have been more generally recognised by professional testers. The difficulties with multiple choice are as follows.

The technique tests only recognition knowledge

If there is a lack of fit between at least some candidates' productive and receptive skills, then performance on a multiple choice test may give a quite inaccurate picture of those candidates' ability. A multiple choice grammar test score, for example, may be a poor indicator of someone's ability to *use* grammatical structures. The person who can identify the correct response in the item above may not be able to produce the correct form when speaking or writing. This is in part a question of construct validity; whether or not grammatical knowledge of the kind that can be demonstrated in a multiple choice test *underlies* the productive use of grammar. Even if it does, there is still a gap to be bridged between knowledge and use; if use is what we are interested in, that gap will mean that test scores are at best giving incomplete information.

Guessing may have a considerable but unknowable effect on test scores

The chance of guessing the correct answer in a three-option multiple choice item is one in three, or roughly thirty-three per cent. *On average* we would expect someone to score 33 on a 100-item test purely by guesswork. We would expect some people to score fewer than that by guessing, others to score more. The trouble is that we can never know what part of any particular individual's score has come about through guessing. Attempts are sometimes made to estimate the contribution of guessing by assuming that all incorrect responses are the result of guessing, and by further assuming that the individual has had average luck in guessing. Scores are then reduced by the number of points the individual is estimated to have obtained by guessing. However, neither assumption is necessarily correct, and we cannot know that the revised score is the same as (or very close to) the one an individual would have obtained without guessing. While other testing methods may also involve guessing, we would normally expect the effect to be much less, since candidates will usually not have a restricted number of responses presented to them (with the information that one of them is correct).

The technique severely restricts what can be tested

The basic problem here is that multiple choice items require distractors, and distractors are not always available. In a grammar test, it may not be possible to find three or four plausible alternatives to the correct structure. The result is that command of what may be an important structure is simply not tested. An example would be the distinction in English between the past tense and the present perfect. Certainly for learners at a certain level of ability, in a given linguistic context, there are no other alternatives that are likely to distract. The argument that this must be a difficulty for *any* item that attempts to test for this distinction is difficult to sustain, since other items that do not overtly present a choice may elicit the candidate's usual behaviour, without the candidate resorting to guessing.

It is very difficult to write successful items

A further problem with multiple choice is that, even where items are possible, good ones are extremely difficult to write. Professional test writers reckon to have to write many more items than they actually need for a test, and it is only after pretesting and statistical analysis of performance on the items that they can recognise the ones that are usable. It is my experience that multiple choice tests that are produced for use within institutions are often shot through with faults. Common amongst these are: more than one correct answer; no correct answer; there are clues in the options as to which is correct (for example the correct option may be different in length to the others); ineffective distractors. The amount of work and expertise needed to prepare good multiple choice tests is so great that, even if one ignored other problems associated with the technique, one would not wish to recommend it for regular achievement testing (where the same test is not used repeatedly) within institutions. Savings in time for administration and scoring will be outweighed by the time spent on successful test preparation. It is true that the development and use of item banks, from which a selection can be made for particular versions of a test, makes the effort more worthwhile, but great demands are still made on time and expertise.

Backwash may be harmful

It should hardly be necessary to point out that where a test which is important to students is multiple choice in nature, there is a danger that practice for the test will have a harmful effect on learning and teaching. Practice at multiple choice items (especially when, as happens, as much attention is paid to improving one's educated guessing as to the content of the items) will not usually be the best way for students to improve their command of a language.

Cheating may be facilitated

The fact that the responses on a multiple choice test (a, b, c, d) are so simple makes them easy to communicate to other candidates nonverbally. Some defence against this is to have at least two versions of the test, the only difference between them being the order in which the options are presented.

All in all, the multiple choice technique is best suited to relatively infrequent testing of large numbers of candidates. This is not to say that there should be *no* multiple choice items in tests produced regularly within institutions. In setting a reading comprehension test, for example, there may be certain tasks that lend themselves very readily to the multiple choice format, with obvious distractors presenting themselves in the text. There are real-life tasks (say, a shop assistant identifying which one of four dresses a customer is describing) which are essentially multiple choice. The simulation in a test of such a situation would seem to be perfectly appropriate. What the reader is being urged to avoid is the excessive, indiscriminate, and potentially harmful use of the technique.

Cloze, C-Test, and dictation: measuring overall ability

The three techniques that are to be discussed in the remainder of this chapter have in common the fact that they seem to offer economical ways of measuring overall ability in a language. The cloze technique has in addition been recommended as a means of measuring reading ability.

During the 1970s there was much excitement in the world of language testing about what was called the 'Unitary Competence Hypothesis'. In brief, this was the suggestion that the nature of language ability was such that it was impossible to break it down into component parts. You could not, for instance, obtain reliable separate measures of a person's reading or listening ability, or of their grammatical or lexical ability. If you attempted to do this, you would find that you were only measuring some central, unitary language ability. A good deal of statistical evidence was presented in support of this hypothesis, but the hypothesis was eventually shown to be false (see the *Further reading* section). As most of us have always believed, not all individual learners of a language show equal mastery of all aspects of performance in that language. A learner may be a highly proficient speaker but a poor writer, or vice versa. It follows from this that if we want to know, for example, how well an individual speaks, then we will not always get accurate information if we base our assessment on his or her performance in writing.

One reason why various studies provided statistical support for the Unitary Competence Hypothesis was that they were concerned with the performance of groups rather than of individuals. Differences *within* individuals (say, between writing and speaking) tended to be hidden by the differences *between* individuals. What is more, for many individuals the differences between abilities were small. In general, where people have had training in both speaking and writing, the better someone writes, the better they are likely to speak. This may reflect at least three facts. First, people differ in their aptitude for language learning; someone with high aptitude will tend to perform above average in all aspects. Secondly, training in the language is often (but not always) such as to encourage comparable development in the different skills. Thirdly, there is likely to be at least some transfer of learning from one skill to another; words learned through listening would seem unlikely to be unavailable to the learner when reading.

It is because of the tendencies described in the previous paragraph that it makes sense to speak of someone being 'good (or quite good, or bad) at a language'. While the Unitary Competence Hypothesis has been abandoned, the notion of overall ability can, in some circumstances, be a useful concept. There are times when all we need is an approximate idea of someone's ability; great accuracy and detailed diagnostic information are not required. These are situations where there is no question of decisions which might have serious adverse effects being taken on the basis of this kind of information. The test results might, for example, be used as a means of placing people in language classes from which they can easily be moved if misplacement has occurred.

One way of measuring overall ability would of course be to measure a variety of separate abilities and then to combine scores. This would hardly be economical if we simply wanted to use test results for making decisions which were not of critical importance. The techniques recommended in the remainder of the chapter have the advantage of being relatively easy to prepare, administer and score. They have also been the subject of quite considerable research, and for that reason we know more about them than many other techniques.

Varieties of cloze procedure

In its original form, the cloze procedure involves deleting a number of words in a passage, leaving blanks, and requiring the person taking the test to attempt to replace the original words. After a short unmutilated 'lead-in', it is usually about every seventh word which is deleted. The following example, which the reader might wish to attempt, was used in research into cloze in the United States (put only one word in each space). The answers are at the end of this chapter.

What is a college?

Confusion exists concerning the real purposes, aims, and goals of a college. What are these? What should a college be?

Some believe that the chief function 1.＿＿＿＿＿ even a liberal arts college is 2.＿＿＿＿＿ vocational one. I feel that the 3.＿＿＿＿＿ function of a college, while important, 4.＿＿＿＿＿ nonetheless secondary. Others profess that the 5.＿＿＿＿＿ purpose of a college is to 6.＿＿＿＿＿ paragons of moral, mental, and spiritual 7.＿＿＿＿＿ – Bernard McFaddens with halos. If they 8.＿＿＿＿＿ that the college should include students 9.＿＿＿＿＿ the highest moral, ethical, and religious 10.＿＿＿＿＿ by precept and example, I 11.＿＿＿＿＿ willing to accept the thesis.

I 12.＿＿＿＿＿ in attention to both social amenities 13.＿＿＿＿＿ regulations, but I prefer to see 14.＿＿＿＿＿ colleges get down to more basic 15.＿＿＿＿＿ and ethical considerations instead of standing in loco parentis 16.＿＿＿＿＿ four years when 17.＿＿＿＿＿ student is attempting in his youthful 18.＿＿＿＿＿ awkward ways, to grow up. It 19.＿＿＿＿＿ been said that it was not 20.＿＿＿＿＿ duty to prolong adolescences. We are 21.＿＿＿＿＿ adept at it.

There are those 22.＿＿＿＿＿ maintain that the chief purpose of 23.＿＿＿＿＿ college is to develop "responsible citizens." 24.＿＿＿＿＿ is good if responsible citizenship is 25.＿＿＿＿＿ by-product of all the factors which 26.＿＿＿＿＿ to make up a college education 27.＿＿＿＿＿ life itself. The difficulty arises from 28.＿＿＿＿＿ confusion about the meaning of responsible 29.＿＿＿＿＿. I know of one college which 30.＿＿＿＿＿ mainly to produce, in a kind 31.＿＿＿＿＿ academic assembly line, outstanding exponents of 32.＿＿＿＿＿ system of free enterprise.

Likewise, I 33.＿＿＿＿＿ to praise the kind of education 34.＿＿＿＿＿ extols one kind of economic system 35.＿＿＿＿＿ the exclusion of the good portions 36.＿＿＿＿＿ other kinds of economic systems. It 37.＿＿＿＿＿ to me therefore, that a college 38.＿＿＿＿＿ represent a combination of all 39.＿＿＿＿＿ above aims, and should be something 40.＿＿＿＿＿ besides – first and foremost an educational 41.＿＿＿＿＿, the center of which is the 42.＿＿＿＿＿ exchange between teachers and students.

I 43.＿＿＿＿＿ read entirely too many statements such 44.＿＿＿＿＿ this one on admissions application papers: "45.＿＿＿＿＿ want a college education because I 46.＿＿＿＿＿ that this will help to support 47.＿＿＿＿＿ and my family." I suspect that 48.＿＿＿＿＿ job as a bricklayer would help this 49.＿＿＿＿＿ to support himself and his family 50.＿＿＿＿＿ better than a college education.

(Oller and Conrad 1971)

Some of the blanks you will have completed with confidence and ease. Others, even if you are a native speaker of English, you will have found difficult, perhaps impossible. In some cases you may have supplied a word which, though different from the original, you may think just as good or even better. All of these possible outcomes are discussed in the following pages.

There was a time when the cloze procedure seemed to be presented almost as a language testing panacea. An integrative method, it was thought by many to draw on the candidate's ability to process lengthy passages of language: in order to replace the missing word in a blank, it was necessary to go beyond the immediate context. In predicting the missing word, candidates made use of the abilities that underlay all their language performance. The cloze procedure therefore provided a measure of those underlying abilities, its content validity deriving from the fact that the deletion of every nth word meant that a representative sample of the linguistic features of the text was obtained. (It would not be useful to present the full details of the argument in a book of this kind. The interested reader is referred to the *Further reading* section at the end of the chapter.) Support for this view came in the form of relatively high correlations between scores on cloze passages and total scores on much longer more complex tests, such as the University of California at Los Angeles (UCLA) English as a Second Language Placement Test (ESLPE), as well as with the individual components of such tests (such as reading and listening).

The cloze procedure seemed very attractive. Cloze tests were easy to construct, administer and score. Reports of early research seemed to suggest that it mattered little which passage was chosen or which words were deleted; the result would be a reliable and valid test of candidates' underlying language abilities (the cloze procedure was also advocated as a measure of reading ability; see Chapter 10).

Unfortunately, cloze could not deliver all that was promised on its behalf. For one thing, as we saw above, even if some underlying ability is being measured through the procedure, it is not possible to predict accurately from this what is people's ability with respect to the variety of separate skills (speaking, writing etc.) in which we are usually interested. Further, it turned out that different passages gave different results, as did the deletion of different sets of words in the same passage. Another matter for concern was the fact that intelligent and educated native speakers varied quite considerably in their ability to predict the missing words. What is more, some of them did less well than many non-native speakers. The validity of the procedure, even as a very general measure of overall ability, was thus brought into question.

There seems to be fairly general agreement now that the cloze procedure cannot be depended upon automatically to produce reliable and useful tests. There is need for careful selection of texts and some pretesting. The fact that deletion of every nth word almost always produces problematical items (for example impossible to predict the missing word), points to the advisability of a careful *selection* of words to delete, from the outset. The following is an in-house cloze passage, for students at university entrance level, in which this has been done.[1] Again the reader is invited to try to complete the gaps.

```
Choose the best word to fill each of the numbered blanks
in the passage below. Write your answers in the space
provided in the right hand margin. Write only ONE word for
each blank.
```

Ecology

```
Water, soil and the earth's green mantle of
plants make up the world that supports the
animal life of the earth. Although modern
man seldom remembers the fact, he could not
exist without the plants that harness the
sun's energy and manufacture the basic food-
stuffs he depends   (1)   for life. Our          1_____
attitude   (2)   plants is a singularly           2_____
narrow   (3)  . If we see any immediate           3_____
utility in   (4)   plant we foster it.            4_____
  (5)   for any reason we find its presence       5_____
undesirable,   (6)   merely a matter of           6_____
indifference, we may condemn   (7)   to           7_____
destruction. Besides the various plants
  (8)   are poisonous to man or to                8_____
  (9)   livestock, or crowd out food plants,      9_____
many are marked   (10)   destruction merely      10_____
because, according to our narrow view, they
happen to   (11)   in the wrong place at the     11_____
  (12)   time. Many others are destroyed         12_____
merely   (13)   they happen to be associates     13_____
of the unwanted plants.

The earth's vegetation is   (14)   of a web      14_____
of life in which there are intimate and
essential relations between plants and the
earth, between plants and   (15)   plants,       15_____
between plants and animals. Sometimes we
have no   (16)   but to disturb                  16_____
  (17)   relationships, but we should            17_____
  (18)   so thoughtfully, with full              18_____
awareness that   (19)   we do may                19_____
  (20)   consequences remote in time and         20_____
place.
```

---

1. Because they see the selection of deletions as fundamentally different from the original cloze procedure, some testers feel the need to give this procedure a new name. Weir (1988a), for instance, refers to this testing method as 'selective deletion gap filling'.

The deletions in the above passage were chosen to provide 'interesting' items. Most of them we might be inclined to regard as testing 'grammar', but to respond to them successfully more than grammatical ability is needed; processing of various features of context is usually necessary. Another feature is that native speakers of the same general academic ability as the students for whom the test was intended could be expected to provide acceptable responses to all of the items. The acceptable responses are themselves limited in number. Scores on cloze passages of this kind in the Cambridge Proficiency Examination have correlated very highly with performance on the test as a whole. It is this kind of cloze that I would recommend for measuring overall ability. General advice on the construction of such tests is given below.

It may reasonably be thought that cloze procedures, since they produce purely pencil and paper tests, cannot tell us anything about the oral component of overall proficiency.[2]

However, some research has explored the possibility of using cloze passages based on tape-recordings of oral interaction to predict oral ability. The passage used in some of that research is presented here. This type of material would not normally be used in a test for non-native speakers as it is very culturally bound, and probably only somebody from a British background could understand it fully. It is a good example of informal family conversation, where sentences are left unfinished and topics run into each other. (Again the reader is invited to attempt to predict the missing words. Note that things like John's, I'm etc. count as one word. Only one word per space.)

Family reunion

Mother:	I love that dress, Mum.
Grandmother:	Oh, it's M and S.
Mother:	Is it?
Grandmother:	Yes, five pounds.
Mother:	My goodness, it's not, Mum.
Grandmother:	But it's made of that T-shirt stuff, so I don't think it'll wash very .... (1), you know, they go all ...
Mother:	sort .... (2) ... I know the kind, yes ...
Grandmother:	Yes.
Mother:	I've got some T-shirts of that, and .... (3) shrink upwards and go wide ...
Grandmother:	I know, so ...

⟫→

---

2. In fact, cloze tests have been administered orally on an individual basis, particularly to younger children – but this is a time-consuming operation and it is not clear that the information it provides is as useful as can be obtained through more usual testing procedures.

Mother:	It's a super colour. It .... (4) a terribly expensive one, doesn't it? .... (5) you think so when you saw .... (6)?
Grandmother:	Well, I always know in Marks. .... (7) just go in there and ... and .... (8) it's not there I don't buy it. I know I won't like anything else. I got about three from there ... four from there. Only I wait about ...
Girl:	Mummy, can I have a sweetie?
Mother:	What, love?
Grandmother:	Do you know what those are called? ... Oh, I used to love them .... (9) I was a little girl. Liquorice comfits. Do you like liquorice? Does she?
Mother:	.... (10) think she quite likes it. Do .... (11)? We've got some liquorice allsorts actually .... (12) the journey.
Grandmother:	Oh yes.
Mother:	And I said she could have one after.
Grandmother:	Oh, I'm going to have one. No, I'm .... (13). No, it'd make me fat, dear.
Mother:	Listen. Do you want some stew? It's hot now.
Grandmother:	No, no, darling. I don't want anything.
Mother:	Don't you want any? Because .... (14) just put it on the table.
Grandmother:	I've got my Limmits.
Mother:	Are you going .... (15) eat them now with us?
Grandmother:	Yes. .... (16) you going to have yours ... yours now?
Mother:	Well, I've just put mine on the plate, but Arth says he doesn't .... (17) any now.
Grandmother:	Oh yes, go on.
Mother:	So ... so he's going to come down later ...
Grandmother:	What are .... (18) going to eat? ... Oh, I like .... (19). Is that a thing that ...
Mother:	... you gave me, but I altered it.
Grandmother:	Did .... (20) shorten it?
Mother:	I took the frill .... (21).
Grandmother:	I thought it looked ...
Mother:	I altered .... (22) straps and I had to ...
Girl:	That's .... (23) you gave me, Granny.... Granny, I'm .... (24) big for that ...
Mother:	And so is Jake. It's for a doll ... Do you remember that?
Grandmother:	No.
Mother:	Oh, Mum, you're awful. .... (25) made it.

Grandmother:	Did I make this beautiful thing? I don't remember making that ... Gosh, I wouldn't make one of those now.
Mother:	I know. You must have ...
Grandmother:	It's, ... (26) know, typical ... no ... I meant a typical Mrs Haversham thing.
Girl:	Can I have a sweetie?
Grandmother:	Harry would ... Carol would be disgusted .... (27) this.
Mother:	Would she?
Grandmother:	Yes, she'd want navy blue or black.
Mother:	Oh.
Grandmother:	Hello, darling ... . (28) can't ... I can't ... I must look .... (29) him a lot, Gemima. Do you .... (30)? I mean Megan. Do you mind?
Girl:	Why?
Grandmother:	Because I have to see who .... (31) like.
Mother:	Mum thinks he looks like Dad ... I mean, Granny thinks ...
Grandmother:	Except of .... (32) he hasn't got his nose, has .... (33)?
Mother:	No, but it doesn't look quite .... (34) big now ... but, ooh, it really .... (35) look enormous when ...
Grandmother:	Oh you darling .... (36) thing. He's got wide eyes, hasn't he? Has he got wide apart eyes?
Mother:	.... (37), I suppose he has, hasn't he?
Grandmother:	I think he's going to be a little like Megan when he gets older ... Yes, I think he is ... Only he's .... (38) dark like she is, is he?
Mother:	Except that his eyes are quite dark, ... (39) they, now ...
Grandmother:	Oh, yes, I think .... (40) bound to go dark, aren't they?
Mother:	Probably, yes.

(Garman and Hughes 1983)

The thinking behind this was that familiarity with the various features of spoken English represented in the text would make a significant contribution to candidates' performance. As it turned out, this 'conversational cloze', administered to overseas students who had already been in Britain for some time, was a better predictor of their oral ability (as rated by their teachers) than was the first cloze passage presented in this chapter. This suggests the possibility of using such a passage as part of a placement test battery of cloze tests, where a direct measure of oral ability is not feasible. More appropriate recordings than the one used in the research could obviously be found.

Advice on creating cloze type passages

1. The chosen passages should be at a level of difficulty appropriate to the people who are to take the test. If there is doubt about the level, a range of passages should be selected for pretesting. Indeed it is always advisable to pretest a number of passages, as their behaviour is not always predictable.
2. The text should be of a style appropriate to the kind of language ability being tested.
3. After a couple of sentences of uninterrupted text, deletions should be made at about every eighth or tenth word (the so called pseudo-random method of deletion). Individual deletions can then be moved a word or two to left or right, to avoid problems or to create interesting 'items'.
4. The passage should then be tried out on a good number of comparable native speakers and the range of acceptable responses determined.
5. Clear instructions should be devised. In particular, it should be made clear what is to be regarded as a word (with examples of *isn't* etc., where appropriate). Students should be assured that no one can possibly replace all the original words exactly. They should be encouraged to begin by reading the passage right through to get an idea of what is being conveyed (the correct responses early in the passage may be determined by later content).
6. The layout of the second test in the chapter (*Ecology*) facilitates scoring. Scorers are given a card with the acceptable responses written in such a way as to lie opposite the candidates' responses.
7. Anyone who is to take a cloze test should have had several opportunities to become familiar with the technique. The more practice they have had, the more likely it is that their scores will represent their true ability in the language.
8. Cloze test scores are not directly interpretable. In order to be able to interpret them we need to have some other measure of ability. If a series of cloze passages is to be used as a placement test (see previous chapter), then the obvious thing would be to have all students currently in the institution complete the passages. Their cloze scores could then be compared with the level at which they are studying in the institution. Information from teachers as to which students could be in a higher (or lower) class would also be useful. Once a pattern was established between cloze test scores and class level, the cloze passages could be used as at least part of the placement procedure.

The C-Test

The C-Test is really a variety of cloze, which its originators claim is superior to the kind of cloze described above. Instead of whole words, it is the second half of every second word which is deleted. An example follows.

> There are usually five men in the crew of a fire engine. One o____ them dri____ the eng____. The lea____ sits bes____ the dri____. The ot____ firemen s____ inside t____ cab o____ the f____ engine. T____ leader h____ usually be____ in t____ Fire Ser____ for ma____ years. H____ will kn____ how t____ fight diff____ sorts o____ fires. S____, when t____ firemen arr____ at a fire, it is always the leader who decides how to fight a fire. He tells each fireman what to do.

(Klein-Braley and Raatz 1984)

The supposed advantages of the C-Test over the more traditional cloze procedure are that only exact scoring is necessary (native speakers effectively scoring 100 per cent) and that shorter (and so more) passages are possible. This last point means that a wider range of topics, styles, and levels of ability is possible. The deletion of elements less than the word is also said to result in a representative sample of parts of speech being so affected. By comparison with cloze, a C-Test of 100 items takes little space and not nearly so much time to complete (candidates do not have to read so much text).

Possible disadvantages relate to the puzzle-like nature of the task. It is harder to read than a cloze passage, and correct responses can often be found in the surrounding text. Thus the candidate who adopts the right puzzle-solving strategy may be at an advantage over a candidate of similar foreign language ability. However, research would seem to indicate that the C-Test functions well as a rough measure of overall ability in a foreign language. The advice given above about the development of cloze tests applies equally to the C-Test (except of course in details of deletion).

Dictation

In the 1960s it was usual, at least in some parts of the world, to decry dictation testing as hopelessly misguided. After all, since the order of words was given, it did not test word order; since the words themselves were given, it did not test vocabulary; since it was possible to identify words from the context, it did not test aural perception. While it might test punctuation and spelling, there were clearly more economical ways of doing this.

At the end of the decade this orthodoxy was challenged. Research revealed high correlations between scores on dictation tests and scores on much longer and more complex tests (such as the UCLA ESLPE). Examination of performance on dictation tests made it clear that words and word order were *not* really *given*; the candidate heard only a stream of sound which had to be decoded into a succession of words, stored, and recreated on paper. The ability to identify words from context was now seen as a very desirable ability, one that distinguished between learners at different levels.

Dictation tests give results similar to those obtained from cloze tests. In predicting overall ability they have the advantage of involving listening ability. That is probably the only advantage. Certainly they are as easy to create. They are relatively easy to administer, though not as easy as the paper-and-pencil cloze. But they are certainly not easy to score. Oller, who was a leading researcher into both cloze and dictation, recommends that the score should be the number of words appearing in their original sequence (misspelled words being regarded as correct as long as no phonological rule is broken). This works quite well when performance is reasonably accurate, but is still time-consuming. With poorer students, scoring becomes very tedious.

Because of this scoring problem, *partial* dictation may be considered as an alternative. In this, part of what is dictated is already printed on the candidate's answer sheet. The candidate has simply to fill in the gaps. It is then clear just where the candidate is up to, and scoring is likely to be more reliable.

Like cloze, dictation may prove a useful technique where estimates of overall ability are needed. The same considerations should guide the choice of passages as with the cloze procedure. The passage has to be broken down into stretches that will be spoken without a break. These should be fairly long, beyond rote memory, so that the candidates will have to decode, store, and then re-encode what they hear (this was a feature of the dictations used in the research referred to above). It is usual, when administering the dictation, to begin by reading the entire passage straight through. Then the stretches are read out, not too slowly, one after the other with enough time for the candidates to write down what they have heard (Oller recommends that the reader silently *spell* the stretch *twice* as a guide to writing time).

In summary, dictation and the varieties of cloze procedure discussed above provide neither direct information on the separate skills in which we are usually interested nor any easily interpreted diagnostic information. With careful application, however, they can prove useful to non-professional testers for purposes where great accuracy is not called for.

READER ACTIVITIES

1. Complete the three cloze passages in the chapter.
   Say what you think each item is testing.
   If there are items for which you cannot provide a satisfactory response, can you explain why?
   Identify items for which there seem to be a number of possible acceptable responses. Can you think of responses which are on the borderline of acceptability? Can you say why they are on the borderline?
2. Choose a passage that is at the right level and on an appropriate topic for a group of students with whom you are familiar. Use it to create tests by:
   - deleting every seventh word after a lead in
   - doing the same, only starting three words after the first deleted word of the first version
   Compare the two versions. Are they equivalent?
   Now use one of them to create a cloze test of the kind recommended.
   Make a C-Test based on the same passage.
   Make a dictation of it too. How do all of them compare?
   If possible administer them to the group of students you had in mind, and compare the results (with each other and with your knowledge of the students).
3. Can you see anything wrong with the following multiple choice items taken from tests written by teachers? What? Try to improve them.

   a) I said to my friend ' .... be stupid.'
           Isn't   Aren't   Didn't   Don't be
   b) What .... you do, if your car broke down?
           must   did   shall
   c) You are too thin. You should eat ....
           many   more   a few
   d) – I'm sorry that the child saw the accident.
        – I don't think it matters. He soon .... it.
           is forgetting   forgets   will forget   will be forgetting
   e) People .... in their reaction to the same stimulus.
           replace   vary   upset   very

Further reading

For all issues discussed in this chapter, including dictation, the most accessible source is Oller (1979). For a more recent treatment of the

Unitary Competence Hypothesis (including Oller's renouncement of it) see Hughes and Porter (1983). The research in which the first cloze passage in the chapter was used is described in Oller and Conrad (1971). Examples of the kind of cloze recommended here are to be found in Cambridge Proficiency Examination past papers. Hughes (1981) is an account of the research into conversational cloze. Streiff (1978) describes the use of oral cloze with Eskimo children. Klein-Braley and Raatz (1984) and Klein-Braley (1985) outline the development of the C-Test. Lado (1961) provides a critique of dictation as a testing technique, while Lado (1986) carried out further research using the passage employed by Oller and Conrad, to cast doubt on their claims. Garman and Hughes (1983) provide cloze passages for teaching, but they could form the basis for tests (native speaker responses given).

Answers to cloze tests

What is a college?   The words deleted from the passage are as follows: 1. of; 2. a; 3. vocational; 4. is; 5. chief; 6. produce; 7. stamina; 8. mean; 9. with; 10. standards; 11. am; 12. believe; 13. and; 14. our; 15. moral; 16. for; 17. the; 18. and; 19. has; 20. our; 21. singularly; 22. who; 23. a; 24. This; 25. a; 26. go; 27. and; 28. a; 29. citizenship; 30. aims; 31. of; 32. our; 33. hesitate; 34. which; 35. to; 36. of; 37. seems; 38. should; 39. the; 40. else; 41. experience; 42. intellectual; 43. have; 44. as; 45. I; 46. feel; 47. me; 48. a; 49. student; 50. much.

Ecology   The words deleted from the passage are as follows: 1. on; 2. to; 3. one; 4. a; 5. If; 6. or; 7. it; 8. which/that; 9. his; 10. for; 11. be; 12. wrong; 13. because; 14. part; 15. other; 16. choice/option; 17. these; 18. do; 19. what; 20. have.

Family reunion   *Acceptable responses*: 1. well; 2. of; 3. they; 4. looks, seems; 5. Did, Didn't; 6. it; 7. I; 8. if; 9. when; 10. I; 11. you; 12. for; 13. not; 14. I've; 15. to; 16. Are; 17. want; 18. you; 19. that; 20. you; 21. off; 22. the; 23. what, one; 24. too; 25. You; 26. you; 27. with, at, by, about; 28. I; 29. at; 30. mind; 31. he's; 32. course; 33. he; 34. as, so, that; 35. did; 36. little, sweet, wee; 37. Yes; 38. not; 39. aren't; 40. they're.

9 Testing writing

We will make the assumption in this chapter that the best way to test people's writing ability is to get them to write.[1]

This is not an unreasonable assumption. Even professional testing institutions are unable to construct indirect tests which measure writing ability accurately (see Chapter 3, *Further reading*; Godshalk *et al.*). And if in fact satisfactory accuracy were a real possibility, considerations of backwash and ease of construction would still argue for the direct testing of writing within teaching institutions.

Given the decision to test writing ability directly, we are in a position to state the testing problem, in a general form for writing. This has three parts:

1. We have to set writing tasks that are properly representative of the population of tasks that we should expect the students to be able to perform.
2. The tasks should elicit samples of writing which truly represent the students' ability.
3. It is essential that the samples of writing can and will be scored reliably.

We shall deal with each of these in turn.

Setting the tasks

Specifying all appropriate tasks and selecting a sample

In order to judge whether the tasks we set are representative of the tasks which we expect students to be able to perform, we have to be clear at the outset just what these tasks are that they should be able to perform. These should be identified in the test specifications. The framework for the specification of content presented in Chapter 7 is relevant here: operations, types of text, addressees, topics.

---

1. We will also assume that the writing of elementary students is not to be tested. Whatever writing skills are required of them can be assessed informally. There seems little point in constructing, for example, a formal test of the ability to form characters or transcribe simple sentences.

Let us look at the specifications for the writing test at the Basic level of the RSA Examination in the Communicative Use of English as a Foreign Language. It should be said immediately that I hold no particular brief for the examining board in question. Indeed I think that there is some conceptual confusion in the content of its specifications for this test. Nevertheless, it represents an unusually thorough attempt to specify test content.

Operations   Expression of thanks
                                requirements
                                opinions
                                comment
                                attitude
                                confirmation
                                apology
                                want/need
                                information

                        Eliciting information
                                directions
                                service
                                (and all areas above)

Text types   *Form*   *Type*

                        Letter   Announcement
                        Postcard   Description
                        Note   Narration
                        Forms   Comment

Addressees   Unspecified except as under topics (below)

Topics   Derived from the following general areas of use:
– social interaction with native and non-native speakers of English
– dealing with official and semi-official bodies
– shopping and using services
– visiting places of interest and entertainment
– travelling and arranging for travel
– using media for information and entertainment
– medical attention and health
– studying for academic/occupational/social purposes

Whatever the conceptual problems, (for instance, the appearance of comment as an operation and as a text type; or the nature of the 'topics') it is probably fair to say that the RSA specifications account for a significant proportion of the writing tasks that students in general language courses which have communicative aims are expected to be able to perform. They ought therefore to be useful to those responsible for testing writing on such courses. Under each heading, institutional testers can identify the elements which apply to their own situation. There will be some points where perhaps more detail is called for; others where additional elements are needed. There is certainly no reason to feel limited to this particular framework or its content, but all in all these specifications should provide a good starting point for many testing purposes.

Once the dimensions of the test have been specified, it becomes relatively straightforward to make a selection in the way outlined in the previous chapter. It is interesting to see how the RSA examiners have done this. One of their examinations at the Basic level is reproduced on pages 78–80.[2]

From this it is clear that the examiners have made a serious attempt to create a representative sample of tasks (the reader might wish to check off the elements in the specification which are represented in the test). What also becomes clear is that with so many *potential* tasks and with so few items, the test's content validity is brought into question. Really good coverage of the range of potential tasks is not possible in a single version of the test. This is a problem to which there is no easy answer. Only research will tell us whether candidates' performance on one small set of selected tasks will result in scores very similar to those that their performance on another small non-overlapping set would have been awarded.

A second example, this time much more restricted, concerns the writing component of a test of English for academic purposes with which I was associated. The purpose of the test was to discover whether a student's written English was adequate for study through the medium of English at a particular overseas university. An analysis of needs had revealed that the most important uses of written English were for the purpose of taking notes in lectures and the writing of examination answers up to two paragraphs in length. The first of these tasks was integrated into the listening component of the test. This left the examination answers. An analysis of examination questions in the university revealed that students were required to describe, explain, compare and contrast, and argue for and against a case. Because in that university the first-year undergraduate course is very general (all students study art, science and social science subjects), almost all reasonably academic topics were appropriate. The addressees were university lecturers, both native speakers and non-native speakers of English.

Using the suggested framework, we can describe the relevant tasks quite succinctly:

Operations   describe, explain, compare and contrast, argue

⋙→ *p.81*

2. Note that the test is intended primarily for candidates living in the United Kingdom.

Testing writing

1. You are in the United Kingdom. You know you will need a cheap air-ticket to visit your home country/take a trip overseas later in the year. You decide to join a travel club so that your journey will be as cheap as possible. Complete the application form below.

'BETATRAVEL TRAVEL CLUB'
The cheapest flights from major UK airports to destinations worldwide.

To join our club you just complete the form. Please complete all sections of the form clearly in ink. Answer all the questions. Do not leave a blank. Put n/a if not applicable. For Section A use BLOCK CAPITALS.

Section A

1. STATE MR., MRS., MISS, MS., or OTHER TITLE...

2. FAMILY NAME...

3. OTHER NAMES...

4. DATE OF BIRTH (write month in letters)...

5. NATIONALITY...

6. PRESENT ADDRESS (incl. post code)...

.... Tel. No. (incl. code)...

7. OCCUPATION...

Section B

8. Which U.K. airport would be most convenient for you?...

9. Which country or countries are you intending to travel to?...

....

10. Proposed date of departure...

Section C Please supply the following further details.

11. Proposed duration of stay outside U.K...

12. Reason for journey...

13. How do you intend to pay for your ticket?...

14. How did you hear of 'Betatravel'?...

Date:

Signature:...

---

2. An English friend of yours living outside the U.K. has given you £10.00 to buy a couple of books for her. She definitely wants "The Guinness Book of Records" and she'd also like a new pocket "Oxford English Dictionary" if the money she has given you is enough.

Write to the bookshop advertised below ordering "The Guinness Book of Records". Find out from them whether £10.00 will be enough also to pay for the dictionary your friend wants. Make sure they send you full details of prices including p & p. Check on what methods of payment they will accept and get them to confirm the latest delivery date (your friend wants the books by the beginning of August).

Write the letter on the next page. Write address(es) on the letter as appropriate.

B.E.B.C.

Britain's leading distributor of English Language Teaching books and aids to students, teachers and booksellers throughout the world.

The Bournemouth English Book Centre,
14 Albion Close, Ringwood Road, Parkstone, Poole BH12 3LL, England
Telephone 0202 736973 (24 hr. answering service). Telex: 418350 BEBOOK G

LE4

Testing writing

3. You are leaving the U.K. for a few weeks. When you arrive at the airport you remember something you forgot to do before leaving home. You can't contact anybody on the phone. Write a brief note to a friend. Apologize for any trouble you are causing. Explain to him what you want him to do. Thank him for helping you.

Write the message and your friend's address on the card below.

4. You've been away for nearly 2 weeks now and you have a lot of news. Write to some English friends who have offered to meet you at the airport on your return. Thank them for the offer. Tell them when and where they can meet you. Tell them the different things you have seen and done since you left. Say how you feel about your trip so far.

Your letter should not be more than 120 words.

Write the letter below.

Text type   examination answers up to two paragraphs in length

Addressees   native speaker and non-native speaker university lecturers

Topics   any capable of academic treatment

It can be seen that in this case it is not at all difficult to select representative writing tasks. Content validity is less of a problem than with the much wider-ranging RSA examination. Since it is only under the heading of 'operations' that there is any significant variability, a test that required the student to write four answers could cover the whole range of tasks, assuming that differences of topic really did not matter. In fact, the writing component of each version of the test contained two writing tasks, and so fifty per cent of all tasks were to be found in each version of the test. The assumption about topics may seem hard to accept. However, topics were chosen with which it was expected all students would be familiar, and information or arguments were provided (see example, page 85).

Obtaining samples that properly represent each candidate's ability

SET AS MANY TASKS AS IS FEASIBLE

We should begin by recognising that from the point of view of validity, the ideal test would be one which required candidates to perform *all* the relevant potential writing tasks. The total score obtained on that test would be our best estimate of a candidate's ability. That total score would be the sum of the scores on each of the different tasks. We would not expect all of those scores to be equal, even if they were perfectly scored on the same scale. First, as we saw in Chapter 5, people's performance on the *same* task is not consistent. For this reason we have to offer candidates as many 'fresh starts' as possible, and each task can represent a fresh start. Secondly, people will simply be better at some tasks than others. If we happen to choose just the task or tasks that a candidate is particularly good at, then the outcome is likely to be very different from that which would result from the ideal test that included all the tasks. Again, this is a reason for including as many different tasks as possible.

Of course, this has to be balanced against practicality; otherwise we would always include all of the potential tasks. It must be remembered, however, that if we need to know something accurate and meaningful about a person's writing ability, then we have to be prepared to pay for that information. What we decide to do will depend in large part on how accurate the information has to be. If it is a matter of placing students in classes from which they can easily be moved to another more appropriate one, then accuracy is not so important; we may be satisfied with a single sample of writing. But if the result is going to be important to candidates – if it could, for example, determine whether they are allowed to study overseas – then certainly more than one sample is necessary if serious injustices are not to be perpetrated.

TEST ONLY WRITING ABILITY, AND NOTHING ELSE

This assumes that we do not want to test other things. In language testing we are not normally interested in knowing whether students are creative, imaginative, or even intelligent, have wide general knowledge, or have good reasons for the opinions they happen to hold. For that reason we should not set tasks which measure these abilities. Look at the following tasks which, though invented, are based on others taken from well-known tests.

1. Write the conversation you have with a friend about the holiday you plan to have together.
2. You spend a year abroad. While you are there, you are asked to talk to a group of young people about life in your country. Write down what you would say to them.
3. 'Envy is the sin which most harms the sinner.' Discuss.
4. The advantages and disadvantages of being born into a wealthy family.

The first task seems to make demands on creativity, imagination, and indeed on script-writing ability. Success at the second would seem to depend to at least some extent on the ability to give talks. It is in fact hard to imagine either of the tasks being derived from a careful specification of writing tasks.

The third and fourth tasks clearly favour candidates who have, or can instantly create, an ordered set of arguments on any topic which they meet. A clear indication that not only language ability is being tested is the fact that many educated native speakers (including me) would not be confident of completely satisfying the examiners. Francis Bacon might have done well, if his answers were not thought too brief.

Another ability which at times interferes with the accurate measurement of writing ability is that of *reading*. While it is perfectly acceptable to expect the candidate to be able to read simple instructions, care has to be taken not to make these so difficult that they cannot be fully understood by everyone whose ability is of sufficiently high standard otherwise to perform adequately on the writing task.

Nor should the instructions be too long. The following item may be thought to suffer from both these faults.

Answer **ONE** of the following questions in **about 250 words**:

Either (a) You've been asked to contribute an article to an international magazine which is running a series called "A Good Read". Write, for the magazine, a review of a book you like.

Or (b) You have recently heard that each year the Axtel Corporation offers the opportunity for a small number of people to spend between three and six months working in one of their offices in Australia, New Zealand, the United States, or Britain. The aim of the scheme is to promote international understanding, and to foster an awareness of different working methods.

Candidates for the scheme are asked to write an initial letter of application, briefly outlining their general background and, more importantly, giving the reasons why they feel they would benefit from the scheme. In addition, they should indicate in which country they would like to work. On the basis of this letter they may be invited for interview and offered a post.

Write the letter of application.

One way of reducing dependence on the candidates' ability to read is to make use of illustrations. The following is from the Joint Matriculation Board's Test in English (Overseas).

The diagram below shows three types of bee.

Compare and contrast the three bees.
Write about three-quarters of a page.

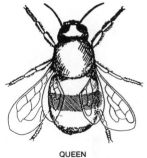

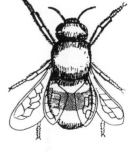

QUEEN   WORKER   DRONE

Testing writing

A series of pictures can be used to elicit a narrative.

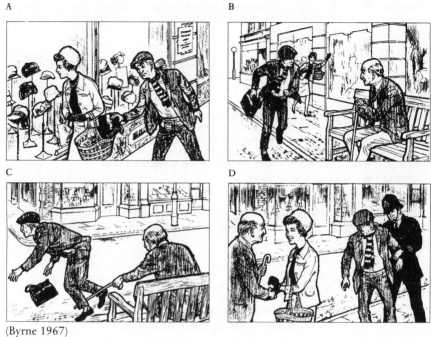

(Byrne 1967)

This may take the form of quite realistic transfer of information.

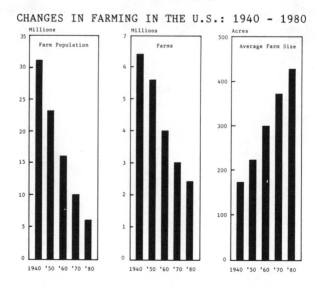

Suppose you are writing a report in which you must
interpret the three graphs shown above. Write the section
of that report in which you discuss how the graphs are
related to each other and explain the conclusions you
have reached from the information in the graphs. Be sure
the graphs support your conclusions.

THIS SPACE MAY BE USED FOR NOTES.

(Reprinted by permission of Educational Testing Service)

RESTRICT CANDIDATES

This echoes the general point made in Chapter 5. The question above
about envy for example, could result in very different answers from the
same person on different occasions. There are so many significantly
different ways of developing a response to the stimulus. Writing tasks
should be well defined: candidates should know just what is required of
them, and they should not be allowed to go too far astray. A useful device
is to provide information in the form of notes (or pictures, as above).

The following example, slightly modified, was used in the test I was
concerned with, mentioned earlier in the chapter.

Compare the benefits of a university education in English with its
drawbacks. Use all of the points given below and come to a
conclusion. You should write about one page.

a) Arabic
   1. Easier for students
   2. Easier for most teachers
   3. Saves a year in most cases

b) English
   1. Books and scientific sources mostly in English
   2. English international language – more and better job
      opportunities
   3. Learning second language part of education/culture

Care has to be taken when notes are given not to provide students with
too much of what they need in order to carry out the task. Full sentences
are generally to be avoided, particularly where they can be incorporated
into the composition with little or no change.

85

Setting tasks which can be reliably scored

In fact a number of the suggestions made to obtain performance that is representative will also facilitate reliable scoring.

SET AS MANY TASKS AS POSSIBLE

The more scores that scorers provide for each candidate, the more reliable should be the total score.

RESTRICT CANDIDATES

The greater the restrictions imposed on the candidates, the more directly comparable will be the performances of different candidates.

GIVE NO CHOICE OF TASKS

Making the candidates perform all tasks also makes comparisons between candidates easier.

ENSURE LONG ENOUGH SAMPLES

The samples of writing which are elicited have to be long enough for judgements to be made reliably. This is particularly important where diagnostic information is sought. For example, in order to obtain reliable information on students' organisational ability in writing, the pieces have to be long enough for organisation to reveal itself. Given a fixed period of time for the test, there is an almost inevitable tension between the need for length and the need to have as many samples as possible.

Obtaining reliable scoring of writing

So far in this chapter we have been concerned to obtain appropriate and reliable samples of writing which will be easy to score reliably. We turn now to the process of scoring. This can be either holistic or analytic.

HOLISTIC SCORING

Holistic scoring (often referred to as 'impressionistic' scoring) involves the assignment of a single score to a piece of writing on the basis of an overall impression of it. This kind of scoring has the advantage of being very rapid. Experienced scorers can judge a one-page piece of writing in just a couple of minutes or even less (scorers of the new TOEFL Test of Written English will apparently have just one and a half minutes for each scoring of a composition). This means that it is possible for each piece of work to be scored more than once, which is fortunate, since it is also *necessary*! Harris (1968) refers to research in which, when each student wrote one 20-minute composition, scored only once, the reliability coefficient was only 0.25. If well conceived and well organised, holistic scoring in which each student's work is scored by four different trained scorers can result in high scorer reliability. There is nothing magical about the number 'four'; it is simply that research has quite consistently shown acceptably high scorer reliability when writing is scored four times.

A reservation was expressed above about the need for such scoring to be well conceived. Not every scoring system will give equally reliable results. The system has to be appropriate to the level of the candidates and the purpose of the test. Look at the following scoring system used in the English-medium university already referred to in this chapter.

NS	Native speaker standard
NS–	Close to native speaker standard
MA	Clearly more than adequate
MA–	Possibly more than adequate
A	ADEQUATE FOR STUDY AT THIS UNIVERSITY
D	Doubtful
NA	Clearly not adequate
FBA	Far below adequacy

This worked perfectly well in the situation for which it was designed. The purpose of the writing component of the test was to determine whether a student's writing ability was adequate for study in English in that university. The standards set were based on an examination of undergraduate students' written work and their teachers' judgements as to the acceptability of the English therein. With students writing two compositions, each independently scored twice, using the above scale, scorer reliability was 0.9. This is about as high as one is likely to achieve in ordinary circumstances (i.e. not in some kind of experiment or research where practicality is of no importance). It was designed for a specific purpose and obviously it would be of little use in most other circumstances. Testers have to be prepared to modify existing scales to suit their own purposes. Look now at the following banding system. This too concerns entry to university level education, this time in Britain. It is in fact a draft of a revised scale for the British Council's ELTS test.

9   The writing displays an ability to communicate in a way which gives the reader full satisfaction. It displays a completely logical organizational structure which enables the message to be followed effortlessly. Relevant arguments are presented in an interesting way, with main ideas prominently and clearly stated, with completely effective supporting material; arguments are effectively related to the writer's experience or views. There are no errors of

D

vocabulary, spelling, punctuation or grammar and the writing shows an ability to manipulate the linguistic systems with complete appropriacy.

8   The writing displays an ability to communicate wit' ᵓut causing the reader any difficulties. It displays a logical organizational structure which enables the message to be followed easily. Relevant arguments are presented in an interesting way, with main ideas highlighted, effective supporting material and they are well related to the writer's own experience or views. There are no significant errors of vocabulary, spelling, punctuation or grammar and the writing reveals an ability to manipulate the linguistic systems appropriately.

7   The writing displays an ability to communicate with few difficulties for the reader. It displays good organizational structure which enables the message to be followed without much effort. Arguments are well presented with relevant supporting material and an attempt to relate them to the writer's experience or views. The reader is aware of but not troubled by occasional minor errors of vocabulary, spelling, punctuation or grammar, and/or some limitations to the writer's ability to manipulate the linguistic systems appropriately.

6   The writing displays an ability to communicate although there is occasional strain for the reader. It is organized well enough for the message to be followed throughout. Arguments are presented but it may be difficult for the reader to distinguish main ideas from supporting material; main ideas may not be supported; their relevance may be dubious; arguments may not be related to the writer's experience or views. The reader is aware of errors of vocabulary, spelling, punctuation or grammar, and/or limited ability to manipulate the linguistic systems appropriately, but these intrude only occasionally.

5   The writing displays an ability to communicate although there is often strain for the reader. It is organized well enough for the message to be followed most of the time. Arguments are presented but may lack relevance, clarity, consistency or support; they may not be related to the writer's experience or views. The reader is aware of errors of vocabulary, spelling, punctuation or grammar which intrude frequently, and of limited ability to manipulate the linguistic systems appropriately.

4   The writing displays a limited ability to communicate which puts strain on the reader throughout. It lacks a clear organizational structure and the message is difficult to follow. Arguments are inadequately presented and supported; they may be irrelevant; if the writer's experience or views are presented their relevance may be difficult to see. The control of vocabulary, spelling, punctuation and grammar is inadequate, and the writer displays inability to manipulate the linguistic systems appropriately, causing severe strain for the reader.

3   The writing does not display an ability to communicate although meaning comes through spasmodically. The reader cannot find any organizational structure and cannot follow a message. Some elements of information are present but the reader is not provided

with an argument, or the argument is mainly irrelevant. The reader is primarily aware of gross inadequacies of vocabulary, spelling, punctuation and grammar; the writer seems to have no sense of linguistic appropriacy, although there is evidence of sentence structure.

2   The writing displays no ability to communicate. No organizational structure or message is recognizable. A meaning comes through occasionally but it is not relevant. There is no evidence of control of vocabulary, spelling, punctuation or grammar, and no sense of linguistic appropriacy.

1   A true non-writer who has not produced any assessable strings of English writing. An answer which is wholly or almost wholly copied from the input text or task is in this category.

0   Should only be used where a candidate did not attend or attempt this part of the test in any way (i.e., did not submit an answer paper with his/her name and candidate number written on).

The British Council 1986

As can be seen, in this case there are nine bands, each one having a description of the writer at each level. Band 7 is a not untypical standard demanded for entry into British universities. These descriptions have two advantages. First, they may help the scorer assign candidates to bands accurately. Secondly, they make the band scores more meaningful to the people (including the students themselves) to whom they may be reported.

If the descriptions become too detailed, however, a problem arises. Look at the following, which is part of the ACTFL (American Council for the Teaching of Foreign Languages) provisional descriptors for writing, and represents an attempt to provide external criteria against which foreign language learning in schools and colleges can be assessed.

Novice–Low	No functional ability in writing the foreign language.
Novice–Mid	No practical communicative writing skills. Able to copy isolated words or short phrases. Able to transcribe previously studied words or phrases.
Novice–High	Able to write simple fixed expressions and limited memorized material. Can supply information when requested on forms such as hotel registrations and travel documents. Can write names, numbers, dates, one's own nationality, addresses, and other simple biographic information, as well as learned vocabulary, short phrases, and simple lists. Can

write all the symbols in an alphabetic or syllabic system or 50 of the most common characters. Can write simple memorized material with frequent misspellings and inaccuracies.

Intermediate–Low

Has sufficient control of the writing system to meet limited practical needs. Can write short messages, such as simple questions or notes, postcards, phone messages, and the like within the scope of limited language experience. Can take simple notes on material dealing with very familiar topics although memory span is extremely limited. Can create statements or questions within the scope of limited language experience. Material produced consists of recombinations of learned vocabulary and structures into simple sentences. Vocabulary is inadequate to express anything but elementary needs. Writing tends to be a loosely organized collection of sentence fragments on a very familiar topic. Makes continual errors in spelling, grammar, and punctuation, but writing can be read and understood by a native speaker used to dealing with foreigners. Able to produce appropriately some fundamental sociolinguistic distinctions in formal and familiar style, such as appropriate subject pronouns, titles of address and basic social formulae.

Intermediate–Mid

Sufficient control of writing system to meet some survival needs and some limited social demands. Able to compose short paragraphs or take simple notes on very familiar topics grounded in personal experience. Can discuss likes and dislikes, daily routine, everyday events, and the like. Can express past time, using content words and time expressions, or with sporadically accurate verbs. Evidence of good control of basic constructions and inflections such as subject-verb agreement, noun-adjective agreement, and straightforward syntactic constructions in present or future time, though errors occasionally occur. May make frequent errors, however, when venturing beyond current level of linguistic competence. When resorting to a dictionary, often is unable to identify appropriate vocabulary, or uses dictionary entry in uninflected form.

Intermediate–High

Sufficient control of writing system to meet most survival needs and limited social demands. Can take notes in some detail on familiar topics, and respond to personal questions using elementary vocabulary and common structures. Can write simple letters, brief synopses and paraphrases, summaries of biographical data and work experience, and short compositions on familiar topics. Can create sentences and short paragraphs relating to most survival needs (food, lodging, transportation, immediate surroundings and situations) and limited social demands. Can relate personal history, discuss topics such as daily life, preferences, and other familiar material. Can express fairly accurately present and future time. Can produce some past verb forms, but not always accurately or with correct usage. Shows good control of elementary vocabulary and some control of basic syntactic patterns but major errors still occur when expressing more complex thoughts. Dictionary usage may still yield incorrect vocabulary of forms, although can use a dictionary to advantage to express simple ideas. Generally cannot use basic cohesive elements of discourse to advantage such as relative constructions, subject pronouns, connectors, etc. Writing, though faulty, is comprehensible to native speakers used to dealing with foreigners.

The descriptions imply a pattern of development common to all language learners. They assume that a particular level of grammatical ability will always be associated with a particular level of lexical ability. This is, to say the least, highly questionable. The potential lack of fit in individuals between performance in the various subskills leads naturally to a consideration of analytic methods of scoring.

ANALYTIC METHODS OF SCORING

Methods of scoring which require a separate score for each of a number of aspects of a task are said to be analytic. The following scale, devised by John Anderson, is based on an oral ability scale found in Harris (1968).

Grammar

__6. Few (if any) noticeable errors of grammar or word order.

__5. Some errors of grammar or word order which do not, however, interfere with comprehension.

__4. Errors of grammar or word order fairly frequent; occasional re-reading necessary for full comprehension.

__3. Errors of grammar or word order frequent; efforts of interpretation sometimes required on reader's part.

__2. Errors of grammar or word order very frequent; reader often has to rely on own interpretation.

__1. Errors of grammar or word order so severe as to make comprehension virtually impossible.

Vocabulary

__6. Use of vocabulary and idiom rarely (if at all) distinguishable from that of educated native writer.

__5. Occasionally uses inappropriate terms or relies on circumlocutions; expression of ideas hardly impaired.

__4. Uses wrong or inappropriate words fairly frequently; expression of ideas may be limited because of inadequate vocabulary.

__3. Limited vocabulary and frequent errors clearly hinder expression of ideas.

__2. Vocabulary so limited and so frequently misused that reader must often rely on own interpretation.

__1. Vocabulary limitations so extreme as to make comprehension virtually impossible.

Mechanics

__6. Few (if any) noticeable lapses in punctuation or spelling.

__5. Occasional lapses in punctuation or spelling which do not, however, interfere with comprehension.

__4. Errors in punctuation or spelling fairly frequent; occasional re-reading necessary for full comprehension.

__3. Frequent errors in spelling or punctuation; lead sometimes to obscurity.

__2. Errors in spelling or punctuation so frequent that reader must often rely on own interpretation.

__1. Errors in spelling or punctuation so severe as to make comprehension virtually impossible.

Fluency (style and ease of communication)

__6. Choice of structures and vocabulary consistently appropriate; like that of educated native writer.
__5. Occasional lack of consistency in choice of structures and vocabulary which does not, however, impair overall ease of communication.
__4. 'Patchy', with some structures or vocabulary items noticeably inappropriate to general style.
__3. Structures or vocabulary items sometimes not only inappropriate but also misused; little sense of ease of communication.
__2. Communication often impaired by completely inappropriate or misused structures or vocabulary items.
__1. A 'hotch-potch' of half-learned misused structures and vocabulary items rendering communication almost impossible.

Form (organisation)

__6. Highly organised; clear progression of ideas well linked; like educated native writer.
__5. Material well organised; links could occasionally be clearer but communication not impaired.
__4. Some lack of organisation; re-reading required for clarification of ideas.
__3. Little or no attempt at connectivity, though reader can deduce some organisation.
__2. Individual ideas may be clear, but very difficult to deduce connection between them.
__1. Lack of organisation so severe that communication is seriously impaired.

SCORE: Gramm:___ + Voc:___ + Mech:___ + Form:___ = ___

There are a number of advantages to analytic scoring. First, it disposes of the problem of uneven development of subskills in individuals. Secondly, scorers are compelled to consider aspects of performance which they might otherwise ignore. And thirdly, the very fact that the scorer has to give a number of scores will tend to make the scoring more reliable. While it is doubtful that scorers can judge each of the aspects independently of the others (there is what is called a 'halo effect'), the mere fact of having (in this case) five 'shots' at assessing the student's performance should lead to greater reliability.

In Anderson's scheme, each of the components is given equal weight. In other schemes, the relative importance of the different aspects, as perceived by the tester (with or without statistical support), is reflected in weightings attached to the various components. Grammatical accuracy, for example, might be given greater weight than accuracy of spelling. A candidate's total score is the sum of the weighted scores.

The main disadvantage of the analytic method is the time that it takes. Even with practice, scoring will take longer than with the holistic method. Particular circumstances will determine whether the analytic method or the holistic method will be the more economical way of obtaining the required level of scorer reliability.

A second disadvantage is that concentration on the different aspects may divert attention from the overall effect of the piece of writing. Inasmuch as the whole is often greater than the sum of its parts, a composite score may be very reliable but not valid. Indeed the aspects which are scored separately (the 'parts'), presumably based on the theory of linguistic performance that most appeals to the author of any particular analytic framework, may not in fact represent the complete, 'correct' set of such aspects. To guard against this, an additional, impressionistic score on each composition is sometimes required of scorers, with significant discrepancies between this and the analytic total being investigated.

It is worth noting a potential problem in Anderson's scale. This arises from the conjunction of frequency of error and the effect of errors on communication. It is not necessarily the case that the two are highly correlated. A small number of grammatical errors of one kind could have a much more serious effect on communication than a large number of another kind. The British Council's recently introduced analytic scale, reproduced below, avoids this difficulty. Note how the descriptions at each level for each component permit the ready provision of diagnostic information. Indeed at Edinburgh University (where the scale was developed) a system has been devised whereby students taking the test can receive a letter which describes their performance on each component, the letter being generated by computer from the score on each component. Of course such diagnosis will be effective only if the samples of writing are sufficiently long for each aspect to be judged reliably.

Appendix D

New Profile Scale and Profile Method 2 ("PM2")

	Communicative Quality	Organization	Argumentation	Linguistic Accuracy	Linguistic Appropriacy
9	The writing displays an ability to communicate in a way which gives the reader full satisfaction.	The writing displays a completely logical organizational structure which enables the message to be followed effortlessly.	Relevant arguments are presented in an interesting way, with main ideas prominently and clearly stated, with completely effective supporting material; arguments are effectively related to the writer's experience or views.	The reader sees no errors of vocabulary, spelling, punctuation or grammar.	There is an ability to manipulate the linguistic systems with complete appropriacy.
8	The writing displays an ability to communicate without causing the reader any difficulties.	The writing displays a logical organizational structure which enables the message to be followed easily.	Relevant arguments are presented in an interesting way, with main ideas highlighted, effective supporting material and they are well related to the writer's own experience or views.	The reader sees no significant errors of vocabulary, spelling, punctuation or grammar.	There is an ability to manipulate the linguistic systems appropriately.
7	The writing displays an ability to communicate with few difficulties for the reader.	The writing displays good organizational structure which enables the message to be followed without such effort.	Arguments are well presented with relevant supporting material and an attempt to relate them to the writer's experience or views.	The reader is aware of but not troubled by occasional minor errors of vocabulary, spelling, punctuation or grammar.	There are minor limitations to the ability to manipulate to linguistic systems appropriately which do not intrude on the reader.
6	The writing displays an ability to communicate although there is occasional strain for the reader.	The writing is organized well enough for the message to be followed throughout.	Arguments are presented but it may be difficult for the reader to distinguish main ideas from supporting material; main ideas may not be supported; their relevance may be dubious; arguments may not be related to the writer's experience or views.	The reader is aware of errors of vocabulary, spelling, punctuation or grammar, but these occasionally.	There is limited ability to manipulate the linguistic systems appropriately, but this intrudes only occasionally.

	Communicative Quality	Organization	Argumentation	Linguistic Accuracy	Linguistic Appropriacy
5	The writing displays an ability to communicate although there is often strain for the reader.	The writing is organized well enough for the message to be followed most of the time.	Arguments are presented but may lack relevance, clarity, consistency or support; they may not be related to the writer's experience or views.	The reader is aware of errors of vocabulary, spelling, punctuation or grammar which intrude frequently.	There is limited ability to manipulate the linguistic systems appropriately, which intrudes frequently.
4	The writing displays a limited ability to communicate which puts strain on the reader throughout.	The writing lacks a clear organizational structure and the message is difficult to follow.	Arguments are inadequately presented and supported; they may be irrelevant; if the writer's experience or views are presented their relevance may be difficult to see.	The reader finds the control of vocabulary, spelling, punctuation and grammar inadequate.	There is inability to manipulate the linguistic systems appropriately, which causes severe strain for the reader.
3	The writing does not display an ability to communicate although meaning comes through spasmodically.	The writing has no discernible organizational structure and a message cannot be followed.	Some elements of information are present but the reader is not provided with an argument, or the argument is mainly irrelevant.	The reader is primarily aware of gross inadequacies of vocabulary, spelling, punctuation and grammar.	There is little or no sense of linguistic appropriacy, although there is evidence of sentence structure.
2	The writing displays no ability to communicate.	No organizational structure or message is recognizable.	A meaning comes through occasionally but it is not relevant.	The reader sees no evidence of control of vocabulary, spelling, punctuation or grammar.	There is no sense of linguistic appropriacy.
1	A true non-writer who has not produced any assessable strings of English writing. An answer which is wholly or almost wholly copied from the input text or task is in this category.				

HOLISTIC OR ANALYTIC?

The choice between holistic and analytic scoring depends in part on the purpose of the testing. If diagnostic information is required, then analytic scoring is essential. The choice also depends on the circumstances of scoring. If it is being carried out by a small, well-knit group at a single site, then holistic scoring, which is likely to be more economical of time, may be the most appropriate. But if scoring is being conducted by a heterogeneous, possibly less well trained group, or in a number of different places (the British Council ELTS test, for instance, is scored at a large number of test centres), analytic scoring is probably called for. Whichever is used, if high accuracy is sought, multiple scoring is desirable.

It should go without saying that the rating systems presented in this chapter are meant to serve only as examples. Testers will almost certainly need to adapt them for use in their own situation.

THE CONDUCT OF SCORING

It is assumed that scorers have already been trained with previously written scripts. Once the test is completed, a search should be made to identify 'benchmark' scripts which typify key levels of ability on each writing task (in the case of the English medium university referred to above, these were 'adequate' and 'not adequate'). Copies of these should then be presented to the scorers for an initial scoring. Only when there is agreement on these benchmark scripts should scoring begin.

Each task of each student should be scored independently by two or more scorers (as many scorers as possible should be involved in the assessment of each student's work), the scores being recorded on separate sheets. A third, senior member of the team should collate scores and identify discrepancies in scores awarded to the same piece of writing. Where these are small, the two scores can be averaged; where they are larger, senior members of the team will decide the score. It is also worth looking for large discrepancies between an individual's performance on different tasks. These may accurately reflect his or her performance, but they may also be the result of inaccurate scoring.

It is important that scoring should take place in a quiet, well-lit environment. Scorers should not be allowed to become too tired. While holistic scoring can be very rapid, it is nevertheless extremely demanding if concentration is maintained.

Multiple scoring should ensure scorer reliability, even if not all scorers are using quite the same standard. Nevertheless, once scoring is completed, it is useful to carry out simple statistical analyses to discover if anyone's scoring is unacceptably aberrant.

READER ACTIVITIES

1. Following the advice given in this chapter, construct two writing tasks appropriate to a group of students with whom you are familiar. Carry out the tasks yourself. If possible, get the students to do them as well. Do any of the students produce writing different in any significant way from what you hoped to elicit? If so, can you see why? Would you wish to change the tasks in any way?
2. This activity is best carried out with colleagues. Score the following three short compositions on how to increase tourism, using each of the scales presented in the chapter. Which do you find easiest to use, and why? How closely do you and your colleagues agree on the scores you assign? Can you explain any large differences? Do the different scales place the compositions in the same order? If not, can you see why not? Which of the scales would you recommend in what circumstances?

1. Nowadays a lot of countries tend to develop their tourism's incomes, and therefore trourism called the factory without chemny. Turkey, which undoubtedly needs forign money, trys to increase the number of foreign tourists coming to Turkey. What are likely to do in order to increase this number.

At first, much more and better advertising should do in foreign countries and the information offices should open to inform the people to decide to come Turkey. Secondly, improve facilities, which are hotels, transportation and communecation. Increase the number of hotels, similarly the number of public transportation which, improve the lines of communication. Thirdly which is important as two others is training of personnel. This is also a basic need of tourism, because the tourist will want to see in front of him a skilled guides or a skilled hotel managers. The new school will open in order to train skilled personnel and as well as theoric knowledges, practice must be given them.

The countries which are made available these three basic need for tourists have already improved their tourism's incomes. Spain is a case in point or Greec. Although Turkey needs this income; it didn't do any real attempts to achive it. In fact all of them should have already been done, till today. However it is late, it can be begin without loosing any time.

2 . A nation can't make improvements, if it doesn't let the minds of their
people breathe and expand to understand more about life than what is at the
end of the street, this improvement can be made by means of tourism.

There are several ways to attract more people to our country. First of
all, advertisements and information take an important place. These
advertisements and information should be based on the qualities of that
place without exaggeration. The more time passes and the more information
tourists gather about one country, the more assured they can be that it
will be a good experience. People travel one place to another in order
to spend their holiday, to see different cultures or to attend conferences.
All of these necessitate facilities. It is important to make some points
clear. Hotel, transportation and communication facilities are a case in
point. To some extent, we can minimize the diffeculties by means of money.
Furthermore, this situation does not only depend on the financial situation,
but also behaviors towards the tourists. Especially, a developing country
should kept in mind the challenge of the future rather than the mistakes
of the past, in order to achive this, the ways of training of personnel
may be found. The most important problem faced by many of countries is
whether the decisions that must be made are within the capabilities of
their education system. Educating guides and hotel managers are becoming
more and more important.

As a result, it should once more be said that, we may increase the number
of foreign tourists coming to Turkey by taking some measures. Advertisement,
information, improving facilities and training personnel may be effective,
but also all people should be encouraged to contribute this event.

. Tourism is now becoming a major industry troughout the world. For many
countries their tourist trade is an essential source of their revenue.

All countries have their aim particular atractions for tourists and this
must be kept in mind when advertising Turkey abroad. For example Turkey,
which wants to increase the number of foreign tourists coming must
advertise its culture and sunshine.

>>>→

Improving facilities like hotels, transportation and communication play
important role on this matter more Hotels can be built and avaliable ones
can be kept clean and tidy. New and modern transportation systems must
be given to foreign tourists and one more, the communication system must
work regularly to please these people.

Tourists don't want to be led around like sheep. They want to explore for
themselves and avoid the places which are pact out with many other tourist.
Because of that there must be their trained guides on their towns through
anywhere and on the other hand hotel managers must be well trained. They
must keep being kind to foreign tourist and must know English as well.

If we make tourists feel comfortable im these facts, tourism will increase
and we will benefit from it.

(Hughes *et al.* 1987: 145–7)

3. This activity is also best carried out with colleagues. Construct a
   holistic writing scale and an analytic writing scale appropriate for use
   with the group of students you have already identified. If possible,
   score the students' efforts on the two tasks, using both methods. Look
   at differences between scorers and between methods, as in the
   previous activity. What changes would you make in the scales? Which
   of the two scales would be most useful for your purposes?

Further reading

A very good book on the testing of writing is Jacobs *et al.* (1981). The
background to the new British Council scales is reported in Hamp-Lyons
(1987).

10 Testing oral ability

The assumption is made in this chapter that the objective of teaching spoken language is the development of the ability to interact successfully in that language, and that this involves comprehension as well as production. It is also assumed that at the earliest stages of learning formal testing of this ability will not be called for, informal observation providing any diagnostic information that is needed.

The basic problem in testing oral ability is essentially the same as for testing writing. We want to set tasks that form a representative sample of the population of oral tasks that we expect candidates to be able to perform. The tasks should elicit behaviour which truly represents the candidates' ability and which can be scored validly and reliably.

Setting the tasks

Specifying all appropriate tasks

As in the previous chapter, we shall begin by considering test content. This will be followed by a discussion of criterial levels of performance and of possible test formats.

CONTENT

We can again make use of the framework introduced in Chapter 7: *Operations, Types of text, Addressees,* and *Topics.* RSA test specifications, this time for 'Oral interaction' at the intermediate level, serve as an illustration.

> **Operations** The operation is to take part in oral interaction which may involve the following language functions:
> *Expressing:* thanks, requirements, opinions, comment, attitude, confirmation, apology, want/need, information, complaints, reasons/justifications
> *Narrating:* sequence of events
> *Eliciting:* information, directions, service, clarification, help, permission, (and all areas above)
> *Directing:* ordering, instructing (how to), persuading, advising, warning

Reporting: description, comment, decisions.

Text types dialogue and multi-participant interactions normally of a face-to-face nature but telephone conversations not excluded.

Addressees and topics Not specified except as under 'Topics for writing'.

Criterial levels of performance

The fact that particular grammatical structures are not specified as content, and that there is no reference to vocabulary or pronunciation, does not of course mean that there are no requirements with respect to these elements of oral performance. These would be dealt with separately as part of a statement of criterial levels. Thus for the RSA test at intermediate level:

Accuracy Pronunciation still obviously influenced by L1 though clearly intelligible. Grammatical/lexical accuracy is generally high, though some errors which do not destroy communication are acceptable.

Appropriacy Use of language generally appropriate to function. The overall intention of the speaker is always clear.

Range A fair range of language is available to the candidate. He is able to express himself without overtly having to search for words.

Flexibility: Is able to take the initiative in a conversation and to adapt to new topics or changes of direction – though neither of these may be consistently manifested.

Size Most contributions may be short, but some evidence of ability to produce more complex utterances and to develop these into discourse should be manifested.

The reader may well feel that these descriptions of levels of ability are not sufficiently precise to use with any consistency. In fact, even where specification is more precise than this, the operationalisation of criterial levels has to be carried out in conjunction with samples of candidates' performances.

Another approach to the specification of skills is to combine the elements of content with an indication of criterial levels of ability. The rating scales against which candidates' performances are judged provide the specifications. Examples of these are the ACTFL Guidelines (see pages 89–91) and the Interagency Language Roundtable (ILR) proficiency ratings (which were in fact used in the development of the ACTFL Guidelines). Thus, the ACTFL description of 'Intermediate-Mid' ability:

Intermediate

The Intermediate level is characterised by the speaker's ability to:

- create with the language by combining and recombining learned elements, though primarily in a reactive mode;
- initiate, minimally sustain, and close in a simple way basic communicative tasks; and
- ask and answer questions.

Intermediate–Mid

Able to handle successfully a variety of uncomplicated, basic and communicative tasks and social situations. Can talk simply about self and family members. Can ask and answer questions and participate in simple conversations on topics beyond the most immediate needs, for example personal history and leisure time activities. Utterance length increases slightly, but speech may continue to be characterised by frequent long pauses, since the smooth incorporation of even basic conversational strategies is often hindered as the speaker struggles to create appropriate language forms. Pronunciation may continue to be strongly influenced by first language and fluency may still be strained. Although misunderstandings still arise, the Intermediate-Mid speaker can generally be understood by sympathetic interlocuters.

The ILR description of 'limited working proficiency' (the ILR scales relate to the use of language for a specific purpose, being used for assessing the foreign language ability of US Government agency staff) is as follows:

> Able to satisfy routine social demands and limited work requirements. Can handle with confidence but not with facility most social situations including introductions and casual conversations about current events, as well as work, family, and autobiographical information; can handle limited work requirements, needing help in handling any complications or difficulties; can get the gist of most conversations on non-technical subjects (i.e. topics which require no specialised knowledge) and has a speaking vocabulary sufficient to respond simply with some circumlocutions; accent, though often quite faulty, is intelligible; can usually handle elementary constructions quite accurately but does not have thorough or confident control of the grammar.

It will be seen that the ACTFL and ILR scales are less specific about content. In the case of ILR interviews, some indication of potential content is to be obtained from accounts of the elicitation procedures used by their interviewers. Whatever approach is adopted, the important thing is for the tester to be as clear as possible at the outset (before the test is written) about the nature of the ability that is to be measured.

FORMAT

Listed here are three general formats with brief comments on them. More detailed elicitation procedures are to be found in the next section.

Interview   The most obvious format for the testing of oral interaction is the interview. In its traditional form, however, it has at least one potentially serious drawback. The relationship between the tester and the candidate is usually such that the candidate speaks as to a superior and is unwilling to take the initiative. As a result, only one style of speech is elicited, and many functions (such as asking for information) are not represented in the candidate's performance. Ways of getting round this problem by introducing a variety of techniques into the interview situation are presented in the next section. The word 'interview' is used below in this extended sense.

Interaction with peers   Two or more candidates may be asked to discuss a topic, make plans, and so on. The problem with this is that the performance of one candidate is likely to be affected by that of the others. For example, an assertive and insensitive candidate may dominate and not allow another candidate to show what he or she can do. If this format is used, candidates should be carefully matched whenever possible.

Response to tape-recordings   Uniformity of elicitation procedures can be achieved through presenting all candidates only with the same audio- (or video-) tape-recorded stimuli. This ought to promote reliability. There can also be economy where a language laboratory is available, since large numbers of candidates can be tested at the same time. The obvious disadvantage of this format is its inflexibility: there is no way of following up candidates' responses.

Obtaining a sample that properly represents each candidate's ability and which can be reliably judged

This section begins with general advice and then goes on to suggest techniques for different formats.

ADVICE ON PLANNING AND CONDUCTING ORAL TESTS

1. Make the oral test as long as is feasible. It is unlikely that much reliable information can be obtained in less than about 15 minutes, while 30 minutes can probably provide all the information necessary for most purposes. As part of a placement test, however, a five- or ten-minute interview should be sufficient to prevent gross errors in assigning students to classes.
2. Include as wide a sample of specified content as is possible in the time available. Select what you regard as a representative sample of the specified content and *then* plan how you will elicit the necessary behaviour (this may well demand the use of more than one format).
3. Plan the test carefully. While one of the advantages of individual oral testing is the way in which procedures can be adapted in response to a candidate's performance, the tester should nevertheless have some pattern to follow. It is a mistake to begin, for example, an interview with no more than a general idea of the course that it might take.
4. Give the candidate as many 'fresh starts' as possible. This means a number of things. First, if possible and if appropriate, more than one format should be used. Secondly, again if possible, it is desirable for candidates to interact with more than one tester. Thirdly, within a format there should be as many separate 'items' as possible. Particularly if a candidate gets into difficulty, not too much time should

be spent on one particular function or topic. At the same time, candidates should not be discouraged from making a second attempt to express what they want to say, possibly in different words.

5. Select interviewers carefully and train them. Successful interviewing is by no means easy and not everyone has great aptitude for it. Interviewers need to be sympathetic and flexible characters, with a good command of the language themselves. But even the most apt need training. They can be given advice, shown video recordings of successful interviews, and can carry out interviews themselves which can be recorded to form the basis for critical discussion.

6. Use a second tester for interviews. Because of the difficulty of conducting an interview and of keeping track of the candidate's performance, it is very helpful to have a second tester present. This person can not only give more attention to how the candidate is performing but also elicit performance which they think is necessary in order to come to a reliable judgement. One of the techniques suggested below needs the co-operation of a second tester.

7. Set only tasks and topics that would be expected to cause candidates no difficulty in their own language.

8. Carry out the interview in a quiet room with good acoustics.

9. Put candidates at their ease. Individual oral tests will always be particularly stressful for candidates. It is important to put them at their ease by being pleasant and reassuring throughout. It is specially important to make the initial stages of the test well within the capacities of all reasonable candidates. Interviews, for example, can begin with straightforward requests for personal (but not too personal) details, remarks about the weather, and so on.

Testers should avoid constantly reminding candidates that they are being assessed. In particular they should not be seen to make notes on the candidates' performance during the interview or other activity. For the same reason, transitions between topics and between techniques should be made as natural as possible. The interview should be ended at a level at which the candidate clearly feels comfortable, thus leaving him or her with a sense of accomplishment.

10. Collect enough relevant information. If the purpose of the test is to determine whether a candidate can perform at a certain predetermined level, then, after an initial easy introduction, the test should be carried out at that level. If it becomes apparent that a candidate is clearly very weak and has no chance of reaching the criterion level, then an interview should be brought gently to a close, since nothing will be learned from subjecting her or him to a longer ordeal. Where, on the other hand, the purpose of the test is to see *what* level the

candidate is at, in an interview the tester has to begin by guessing what this level is on the basis of early responses. The interview is then conducted at that level, either providing confirmatory evidence or revealing that the initial guess is inaccurate. In the latter case the level is shifted up or down until it becomes clear what the candidate's level is. A second tester, whose main role is to assess the candidate's performance, can elicit responses at a different level if it is suspected that the principal interviewer may be mistaken.

11. Do not talk too much. There is an unfortunate tendency for interviewers to talk too much, not giving enough talking time to candidates. Avoid the temptation to make lengthy or repeated explanations of something that the candidate has misunderstood.

ELICITATION TECHNIQUES

The appropriateness of each technique will depend upon the specifications of the test. Most of them can be fitted easily within an interview framework.

Questions and requests for information   Yes/no questions should generally be avoided. Various functions (of the kind listed in the RSA specifications above) can be elicited through requests of the kind: 'Can you explain to me how/why …' and 'Can you tell me what you think of …'.

Pictures   Single pictures are particularly useful for eliciting descriptions. Series of pictures (or video sequences) form a natural basis for narration (the series of pictures on page 84, for example).

Role play   Candidates can be asked to assume a role in a particular situation. This allows the ready elicitation of other language functions. There can be a series of brief items, such as:

> A friend invites you to a party on an evening when you want to stay at home and watch the last episode of a television serial. Thank the friend (played by the tester) and refuse politely.

Or there can be a more protracted exchange:

> You want your mother (played by the tester) to increase your pocket money. She is resistant to the idea. Try to make her change her mind.

> You want to fly from London to Paris on 13 March, returning a week later. Get all the information that you need in order to choose your flights from the travel agent (played by the tester).

Role play can be carried out by two candidates with the tester as an observer. For some roles this may be more natural but, as pointed out above, the performance of one candidate may be affected by that of the other. Similarly, the exchange may not follow the pattern predicted by the tester (and so the intended functions may not be elicited).

Interpreting   It is not intended that candidates should be able to act as interpreters (unless that is specified). However, simple interpreting tasks can test both production and comprehension in a controlled way. One of the testers acts as a monolingual speaker of the candidate's native language, the other as a monolingual speaker of the language being tested. Situations of the following kind can be set up:

> The native language speaker wants to invite a foreign visitor to his or her home for a meal. The candidate has to convey the invitation and act as an interpreter for the subsequent exchange.

Comprehension can be assessed when the candidate attempts to convey what the visitor is saying, and indeed unless some such device is used, it is difficult to obtain sufficient information on candidates' powers of comprehension. Production is tested when the candidate tries to convey the meaning of what the native speaker says.

Discussion   Discussions between candidates can be a valuable source of information. These may be discussions of a topic or in order to come to a decision. Thus an example from the RSA (1984):

> There is too much sport on television.
> *or*
> Your school has a substantial budget to spend on improving facilities. The following have been suggested as possible pur-chases for the school.
> 1. Video equipment
> 2. A swimming pool (indoor or outdoor? But how much would this cost?)
> 3. A mini-bus
> 4. Computer equipment
> 5. A sauna
> 6. Any other suggestion
> Discuss the advantages and disadvantages of each suggestion with your partner and try to reach agreement on the most suitable. Make other suggestions if you wish.

This technique suffers from the disadvantages attached to any method that depends on interaction between candidates. While any reasonable number of candidates could be involved in such discussions, restricting the number to two allows the tester the best opportunity of assessing the performance of more diffident candidates. However, at least one national matriculation examination in English uses larger groups.

Tape-recorded stimuli   As was noted earlier in the chapter, circumstances may dictate that oral ability be tested in the language laboratory. A good source of techniques is the ARELS (Association of Recognised English Language Schools) examination in Spoken English and Comprehension. These include:

> Described situations, for example:
> > You are walking through town one day and you meet two friends who you were sure had gone to live in the USA. What do you say?
>
> Remarks in isolation to respond to, for example:
> > The candidate hears, 'I'm afraid I haven't managed to fix that cassette player of yours yet. Sorry.' *or* 'There's a good film on TV tonight.'
>
> Simulated conversation, for example:
> > The candidate is given information about a play which he or she is supposed to want to see, but not alone. The candidate is told to talk to a friend, Ann, on the telephone, and ask her to go to the theatre and answer her questions. The candidate hears:
>
> Ann: Hello. What can I do for you?
> Ann: Hold on a moment. What's the name of the play, and who's it by?
> Ann: Never heard of it. When's it on exactly?
> Ann: Sorry to mention it, but I hope it isn't too expensive.
> Ann: Well which night do you want to go, and how much would you like to pay?
> Ann: OK. That's all right. It'll make a nice evening out. 'Bye.

Note that although what Ann says is scripted, the style of speech is appropriately informal

For all of the above, an indication is given to candidates of the time available (for example ten seconds) in which to respond.

Imitation   Candidates hear a series of sentences, each of which they have to repeat in turn. This obviously does not in itself represent a cross section of the oral skills that we are usually looking for, but there is research evidence that, provided the sentences are not too short (see what was said about dictation in Chapter 8), learners will make the same kind of errors in performing this task as they will when speaking freely. The advantages of this format are the control which can be exercised in choice of structures etc., and its economy. While it might provide sufficient information as part of a placement test, problems in interpretation, as well as a potentially unfortunate backwash effect, militate against giving it a prominent role in achievement or proficiency tests.

TECHNIQUES NOT RECOMMENDED

Prepared monologue   Some examinations require candidates to present a monologue on a topic after being given a few minutes to prepare. If this task were to be carried out in the native language, there would almost certainly be considerable differences between candidates. For this reason, and because leaving the candidate alone to prepare a monologue must create stress, this technique is not recommended.

Reading aloud Again, there will be significant differences in native-speaker performance, and inevitable interference between the reading and the speaking skills.

Obtaining valid and reliable scoring

Scoring will be valid and reliable only if:

Clearly recognisable and appropriate descriptions of criterial levels are written and scorers are trained to use them.[1]
Irrelevant features of performance are ignored.
There is more than one scorer for each performance.

DESCRIBING THE CRITERIAL LEVELS

Descriptions may be holistic (as the ACTFL and ILR scales presented above) or analytic (as for the RSA test). The advantages and disadvantages of the two approaches have already been discussed in the previous chapter. It was said there that it is possible to use one method as a check on the other. An example of this in oral testing is the American FSI (Foreign Service Institute) interview procedure, which requires the two testers concerned in each interview both to assign candidates to a level holistically and to rate them on a six-point scale for each of the following: accent, grammar, vocabulary, fluency, comprehension. These ratings are then weighted and totalled. The resultant score is then looked up in a table which converts scores into the holistically described levels. The converted score should give the same level as the one to which the candidate was first assigned. If not, the testers will have to reconsider whether their first assignments were correct. The weightings and the conversion tables are based on research which revealed a very high level of agreement between holistic and analytic scoring. Having used this system myself when testing bank staff, I can attest to its efficacy. For the reader's interest I reproduce the rating scales and the weighting table. It must be remembered, however, that these were developed for a particular purpose and should not be expected to work well in a significantly different situation without modification. It is perhaps also worth mentioning that the use of a native-speaker standard against which to judge performance has recently come in for criticism in some language testing circles.

---

1. In some cases it may be sufficient for scorers to be provided with recorded exemplars of the various levels.

Proficiency Descriptions

Accent

1. Pronunciation frequently unintelligible.
2. Frequent gross errors and a very heavy accent make understanding difficult, require frequent repetition.
3. "Foreign accent" requires concentrated listening, and mispronunciations lead to occasional misunderstanding and apparent errors in grammar or vocabulary.
4. Marked "foreign accent" and occasional mispronunciations which do not interfere with understanding.
5. No conspicuous mispronunciations, but would not be taken for a native speaker.
6. Native pronunciation, with no trace of "foreign accent."

Grammar

1. Grammar almost entirely inaccurate phrases.
2. Constant errors showing control of very few major patterns and frequently preventing communication.
3. Frequent errors showing some major patterns uncontrolled and causing occasional irritation and misunderstanding.
4. Occasional errors showing imperfect control of some patterns but no weakness that causes misunderstanding.
5. Few errors, with no patterns of failure.
6. No more than two errors during the interview.

Vocabulary

1. Vocabulary inadequate for even the simplest conversation.
2. Vocabulary limited to basic personal and survival areas (time, food, transportation, family, etc.)
3. Choice of words sometimes inaccurate, limitations of vocabulary prevent discussion of some common professional and social topics.
4. Professional vocabulary adequate to discuss special interests; general vocabulary permits discussion of any non-technical subject with some circumlocutions.
5. Professional vocabulary broad and precise; general vocabulary adequate to cope with complex practical problems and varied social situations.
6. Vocabulary apparently as accurate and extensive as that of an educated native speaker.

Testing oral ability

<u>Fluency</u>

1. Speech is so halting and fragmentary that conversation is virtually impossible.
2. Speech is very slow and uneven except for short or routine sentences.
3. Speech is frequently hesitant and jerky; sentences may be left uncompleted.
4. Speech is occasionally hesitant, with some unevenness caused by rephrasing and groping for words.
5. Speech is effortless and smooth, but perceptibly non-native in speech and evenness.
6. Speech on all professional and general topics as effortless and smooth as a native speaker's.

<u>Comprehension</u>

1. Understands too little for the simplest type of conversation.

2. Understands only slow, very simple speech on common social and touristic topics; requires constant repetition and rephrasing.

3. Understands careful, somewhat simplified speech when engaged in a dialogue, but may require considerable repetition and rephrasing.

4. Understands quite well normal educated speech when engaged in a dialogue, but requires occasional repetition or rephrasing.

5. Understands everything in normal educated conversation except for very colloquial or low-frequency items, or exceptionally rapid or slurred speech.

6. Understands everything in both formal and colloquial speech to be expected of an educated native speaker.

112

```
                    WEIGHTING TABLE
                1    2    3    4    5    6              (A)
                ─────────────────────────────    ───────────────

Accent          0    1    2    2    3    4         ───────────────
Grammar         6   12   18   24   30   36         ───────────────
Vocabulary      4    8   12   16   20   24         ───────────────
Fluency         2    4    6    8   10   12         ───────────────
Comprehension   4    8   12   15   19   23         ───────────────

                                                   ───────────────

                                        Total      ───────────────
```

Note the relative weightings for the various components. The total of the weighted scores is then looked up in a table (not reproduced here) which converts it into a rating on a scale 0–5.

(Adams and Frith 1979: 35–8)

Where analytic scales of this kind are used to the exclusion of holistic scales, the question arises (as with the testing of writing) as to what pattern of scores (for an individual candidate) should be regarded as satisfactory. This is really the same problem (though in a more obvious form) as the failure of individuals to fit holistic descriptions. Once again it is a matter of agreeing, on the basis of experience, what failures to reach the expected standard on particular parameters are acceptable.

TRAINING OF SCORERS

It was mentioned earlier in the chapter that the RSA descriptions of performance might not be thought very precise. The workability of such criteria depends on the training of scorers (who are of course usually testers/interviewers too) to recognise what is intended. This is in fact true even for the most precise descriptions. The usual method is to familiarise the scorers with the rating system and then play them (preferably video-) recordings of past interviews etc. which clearly represent different criterial levels (or are clear passes and fails). Once these are consistently identified by the trainees, less clear cases are presented. Only when trainees can be relied upon to score with consistent accuracy should they be entrusted with 'live' scoring.

Something which scorers should be made aware of is the danger of not judging candidates purely on their linguistic ability. It is obvious that scorers should not be influenced by such features as candidates' pleasantness, prettiness, or the cut of their dress. The truth is that these are hard to exclude from one's judgement – but an effort has to be made!

USE OF MORE THAN ONE SCORER

The scoring of oral ability is generally highly subjective. Even with careful training, a single scorer is unlikely to be as reliable as one would wish. If two testers are involved in a (loosely defined) interview, then they can *independently* assess each candidate. If they agree, there is no problem. If they disagree, even after discussion, then a third assessor may be referred to. In such cases it is necessary to have a recording of the session, if the candidate is to be spared the trauma of being called back for a further session. Even where elicitation is highly controlled and there is a detailed scoring key (as in the ARELS examination), independent double scoring is advisable.

Conclusion

The accurate measurement of oral ability is not easy. It takes considerable time and effort to obtain valid and reliable results. Nevertheless, where backwash is an important consideration, the investment of such time and effort may be considered necessary.

Readers are reminded that the appropriateness of content, descriptions of criterial levels, and elicitation techniques used in oral testing will depend upon the needs of individual institutions or organisations.

READER ACTIVITIES

These activities are best carried out with colleagues.

1. For a group of students that you are familiar with, prepare a holistic rating scale (five bands) appropriate to their range of ability. From your knowledge of the students, place each of them on this scale.
2. Choose three methods of elicitation (for example role play, group discussion, interview). Design a test in which each of these methods is used for five to ten minutes.
3. Administer the test to a sample of the students you first had in mind.
4. Note problems in administration and scoring. How would you avoid them?
5. For each student who takes the test, compare scores on the different tasks. Do different scores represent real differences of ability between tasks? How do the scores compare with your original ratings of the students?

Further reading

Shohamy *et al.* (1986) report on the development of a new national oral test which appears to show desirable psychometric qualities and to have beneficial backwash. A recent book devoted to oral testing is Underhill (1987). The American FSI publishes a 'Testing Kit' which provides information on scales and techniques, and includes sample interviews at the various levels (but not in English). The kit is available from: The Superintendent of Documents, US Government Printing Office, Washington DC 20402. Bachman and Savignon (1986) is a critique of the ACTFL oral interview. Information on the ARELS examinations (and past papers with recordings) can be obtained from ARELS Examinations Trust, 113 Banbury Road, Oxford, OX2 6JX.

11 Testing reading

There was a time when it was taken for granted, at least in some circles, that it was more difficult to construct reliable and valid tests of writing and speaking than of reading and listening. In large part this was because the former seemed to depend on notoriously unreliable subjective scoring, while in the case of the latter, objective scoring was both possible and appropriate. This view of the relative difficulty could be quite mistaken. For one thing, we know from the previous chapter that the subjective scoring of writing can be very reliable (and the same is true for the scoring of speaking). For another, the exercising of receptive skills does not necessarily, or usually, manifest itself directly in overt behaviour. When people write and speak, we see and hear; when they read and listen, there will often be nothing to observe. The task of the language tester is to set reading and listening tasks which will result in behaviour that will demonstrate their successful completion. This is by no means simple, as we shall see below.

Specifying what the candidate should be able to do

In order that we should be clear about the population of abilities that we want to test, it is worthwhile specifying these as accurately and completely as possible. Once again the general framework introduced in Chapter 7 can be used. In particular Content (operations, types of text, addressees, and topics) and Criterial levels of performance.

Content

OPERATIONS
These may be at different levels of analysis. Thus, the following may be thought of as macro-skills, directly related either to needs or to course objectives:

- Scanning text to locate specific information
- Skimming text to obtain the gist
- Identifying stages of an argument
- Identifying examples presented in support of an argument

Underlying these are 'micro-skills', such as:

- Identifying referents of pronouns, etc.
- Using context to guess meaning of unfamiliar words
- Understanding relations between parts of text by recognising indicators in discourse, especially for the introduction, development, transition, and conclusion of ideas

Then there is what would be recognised as the exercise of straightforward grammatical and lexical abilities, such as:

- Recognising the significance of the use of the present continuous with future time adverbials
- Knowing that the word 'brother' refers to a male sibling

And finally, low-level operations, like distinguishing between the letters m and n, or b and d.

A book of the present kind is obviously not the place to argue the merits of various models of the foreign-language reading process. Readers will have their own views as to what goes into successful reading, and it is not for me to try to change them. I think it is appropriate, however, to say something about the broad *levels* of reading processes at which testing is most usefully carried out.

It seems to me that information about students' abilities at the lowest level (for example distinguishing between letters) could only be useful for diagnostic purposes, and can be carried out through informal observation. There is no call for formal testing.

Even at a higher level, information on grammatical and lexical ability would only be diagnostic, and in any case could be acquired through tests of grammar and vocabulary, not necessarily as an integral part of a reading test.

Only at the level of what are referred to above as 'micro-skills' do we reach the point where we find serious candidates for inclusion in a reading test. These we can recognise as skills which we might well wish to teach as part of a reading course in the belief that they will promote the development of the particular macro-skills towards which the course is primarily addressed. It follows from this that items testing such micro-skills are appropriate in achievement tests. If there are skills whose development we wish to encourage, then it is right that they should be represented in tests. At the same time, however, an excess of micro-skill test items should not be allowed to obscure the fact that the micro-skills are being taught not as an end in themselves but as a means of improving macro-skills. At least in final (as opposed to progress) achievement tests, the balance of items should reflect the relationship between the two levels of skill. There is in fact a case for having only items which test macro-skills, since the successful completion of these would imply command of the relevant micro-skills. The same would also be true for proficiency tests. This issue is raised again in the section on the writing of items, below.

TYPES OF TEXT

These might include: textbook, novel, magazine, newspaper (tabloid or quality), academic journal, letter, timetable, poem, etc. They might be further specified, for example newspaper report, newspaper advertisement, newspaper editorial.

This list as it stands may be criticised for being conceptually confused because, for instance, a poem could appear in a newspaper. But of course the list is not intended to identify text types for any particular test. Test designers will (or should) know how best to describe the text types for their particular purposes. How they do it is less important than the thoroughness with which they identify relevant types of text.

A second criticism might be that we do not know that the different types of text actually present readers with different tasks. But the fact that we do not know is in fact a reason for wanting a range of them represented in the test. In addition, of course, there is the question of backwash; the appearance in the test of only a limited range of text types will encourage the reading of a narrow range by potential candidates.

It is worth mentioning authenticity at this point. Whether or not authentic texts (intended for native speakers) are to be used will depend at least in part on what it is intended to measure. Note that even at lower levels of ability, with appropriate items, it is possible to use authentic texts. The RSA test of reading, for instance, uses the same extensive text (for example pages from a newspaper) for all three levels of ability (Basic, Intermediate, and Advanced).

ADDRESSEES

These will obviously be related to text types, and it may not be necessary to specify further: for example we know the intended audience for quality newspapers. But textbooks, for instance, could be for schoolchildren or university students.

TOPICS

It may often be appropriate to indicate the range of topics in only very general terms.

Setting criterial levels of performance

In norm-referenced testing our interest is in seeing how candidates perform by comparison with each other. There is no need to specify criterial levels of performance before tests are constructed, or even before they are administered. This book, however, encourages a broadly criterion-referenced approach to language testing. In the case of the testing of writing, as we saw in the previous chapter, it is possible to describe levels of writing ability that candidates have to attain. While this would not satisfy everyone's definition of criterion-referencing, it is very much in the spirit of that form of testing, and would promise to bring the benefits claimed for criterion-referenced testing.

Setting criterial levels for receptive skills is more problematical. Traditional passmarks expressed in percentages (40 per cent? 50 per cent? 60 per cent?) are hardly helpful, since there seems no way of providing a direct interpretation of such a score. To my mind, the best way to proceed is to use the test tasks themselves to define the level. All of the items (and so the tasks that they require the candidate to perform) should be within the capabilities of anyone to whom we are prepared to give a pass. In other words, in order to pass, a candidate should be expected, in principle, to score 100 per cent. But since we know that human performance is not so reliable, we can set the actual cutting point rather lower, say at the 80 per cent level. In order to distinguish between candidates of different levels of ability, more than one test will be required (see Chapter 6).

Setting the tasks

Selecting texts

Successful choice of texts depends ultimately on experience, judgement, and a certain amount of common sense. Clearly these are not qualities that a handbook can provide; practice is necessary. It is nevertheless possible to offer useful advice. While the points may seem rather obvious, they are often overlooked.

1. Keep specifications constantly in mind and try to select as representative a sample as possible. Do not repeatedly select texts of a particular kind simply because they are readily available.
2. Choose texts of appropriate length. Scanning may call for passages of up to 2,000 words or more. Detailed reading can be tested using passages of just a few sentences.
3. In order to obtain acceptable reliability, include as many passages as possible in a test, thereby giving candidates a good number of fresh starts. Considerations of practicality will inevitably impose constraints on this, especially where scanning or skimming is to be tested.
4. In order to test scanning, look for passages which contain plenty of discrete pieces of information.

E

5. Choose texts which will interest candidates but which will not overexcite or disturb them.
6. Avoid texts made up of information which may be part of candidates' general knowledge. It may be difficult not to write items to which correct responses are available to some candidates without reading the passage.
7. Assuming that it is only reading ability which is being tested, do not choose texts which are too culturally laden.
8. Do not use texts which students have already read (or even close approximations to them).

Writing items

The aim must be to write items which will measure the ability in which we are interested, which will elicit reliable behaviour from candidates, and which will permit highly reliable scoring. We have to recognise that the act of reading does not demonstrate its successful performance. We need to set tasks which will involve candidates in providing evidence of successful reading.

POSSIBLE TECHNIQUES

It is important that the techniques used should interfere as little as possible with the reading itself, and that they should not add a significantly difficult task on top of reading. This is one reason for being wary of requiring candidates to write answers, particularly in the language of the text. They may read perfectly well but difficulties in writing may prevent them demonstrating this. Possible solutions to this problem include:

Multiple choice   The candidate provides evidence of successful reading by making a mark against one out of a number of alternatives. The superficial attraction of this technique is outweighed in institutional testing by the various problems enumerated in Chapter 8. This is true whether the alternative responses are written or take the form of illustrations.

Thus, the following is multiple choice:

> Choose the picture (A, B, C, or D) which the following sentence
> describes: The man with a dog was attacked in the street by a woman.

It should hardly be necessary to say that True/False questions, which are to be found in many tests, are simply a variety of multiple choice, with only one distractor and a 50 per cent probability of choosing the correct response by chance! Having a 'not applicable' or 'we don't know' category adds a distractor and reduces the likelihood of guessing correctly to 33 $\frac{1}{3}$ per cent.

Unique answer   Here there is only one possible correct response. This might be a single word or number, or something slightly longer (for example China; China and Japan; The item on the table; 157). The item may take the form of a question, for example:

In which city do the people described in the 'Urban Villagers' live?

Or it may require completion of a sentence, for example:

.... was the man responsible for the first steam railway.

Though this technique meets the criteria laid down above, and is to be recommended, its use is necessarily limited.

Short answer   When unique answer items are not possible, short answer items may be used. Thus:

According to the author, what does the increase in divorce rates show about people's expectations of marriage and marriage partners?

would expect an answer like:

They (expectations) are greater (than in the past).

Guided short answers   The danger with short-answer questions is of course the one referred to above: a student who has the answer in his or her head after reading the relevant part of the passage may not be able to express it well (equally, the scorer may not be able to tell from the response that the student has arrived at the correct answer). Consider the question:

> What changes have taken place in the attitudes of many European universities to different varieties of English?

Even without knowing the intended answer one suspects that it may create problems of production unrelated to reading ability. The relevant part of the text is as follows (note that the abbreviations 'EngEng' and 'NAmEng' are explained earlier in the text):

> Until recently, many European universities and colleges not only taught EngEng but actually *required* it from their students; i.e. other varieties of standard English were not allowed. This was the result of a conscious decision, often, that some norm needed to be established and that confusion would arise if teachers offered conflicting models. Lately, however, many universities have come to relax this requirement, recognising that their students are as likely (if not more likely) to encounter NAmEng as EngEng, especially since some European students study for a time in North America. Many universities therefore now permit students to speak and write *either* EngEng *or* NAmEng, *so long as they are consistent.*
>
> (Trudgill and Hannah 1982:2)

In such cases the desired response can be obtained by framing the item so that the candidates have only to complete sentences presented to them:

> Complete the following, which is based on the fourth paragraph of the passage.
> 'Many universities in Europe used to insist that their students speak and write only .... Now many of them accept .... as an alternative, but not a .... of the two.'

Summary cloze   A reading passage is summarised by the tester, and then gaps are left in the summary for completion by the candidate. This is really an extension of the guided short answer technique and shares its qualities. It permits the setting of several reliable but relevant items on a relatively short passage. Here is an example:

Original passage

THE GOVERNMENT'S first formal ack-
nowledgement that inhaling other people's
tobacco smoke can cause lung cancer led
to calls yesterday for legislation to make
non-smoking the norm in offices, factories | 5
and public places.

The Government's Independent Scientific Committee on Smoking and Health
concluded that passive smoking was con-
sistent with an increase in lung cancer of | 10
between 10 and 30 per cent in non-
smokers. While the home was probably an
important source of tobacco smoke expo-
sure particularly for the young, "work and
indoor leisure environments with their | 15
greater time occupancy may be more
important for adults", the committee said.

The Department of Health said the
findings were consistent with 200 to 300
lung cancer deaths a year in non-smokers | 20
and some deaths from other smoking-
related diseases such as bronchitis. The
risk had been estimated at about 100 times
greater than the risk of lung cancer from
inhaling asbestos over 20 years in the | 25
amounts in which it is usually found in
buildings.

The findings are to be used by the Health
Education Council to drive home the mes-
sage that passive smoking is accepted as | 30
causing lung cancer. The Government
should encourage proprietors of all public
places to provide for clean air in all
enclosed spaces, the council said, and
legislation should not be ruled out. | 35

Action on Smoking and Health went
further, saying legislation was essential to
make non-smoking the norm in public
places. "In no other area of similar risk to
the public does the Government rely on | 40
voluntary measures," David Simpson, the
director of ASH said.

The Department of Health said concern
over passive smoking had risen in part
through better insulation and draught | 45
proofing. But ministers believed the best
way to discourage smoking was by persua-
sion rather than legislation.

The committee's statement came in an
interim report. Its full findings are due | 50
later this year.

Norman Fowler, the Secretary of State
for Social Services, said it would be for the
new Health Education Authority, which
will replace the Health Education Council | 55
at the end of the month, to take account of
the committee's work.

(Timmins 1987)

Passage with gaps for candidate to complete:

> The Independent Scientific Committee on Smoking and Health has just issued an interim report. It says that _____ smoking (that is, breathing in other people's _____ smoke) is consistent with an increase in _____ of between 10 and 30 per cent amongst people who do not _____. The risk of getting the disease in this way is reckoned to be very much greater than that of getting it through breathing in typical amounts of _____ over long periods of time. Children might be subjected to significant amounts of tobacco smoke at _____, but for _____ places of work and indoor leisure might be more important.
>
> In response to the report, the Health Education Council (which is soon to be _____ by the Health Education Authority) said that the Government should encourage owners of _____ places to ensure that the _____ in all enclosed spaces is clean. Action on Smoking and Health said that _____ was necessary. However, it is known that government ministers would prefer to use _____.

Information transfer   One way of minimising demands on candidates' writing ability is to require them to show successful completion of a reading task by supplying simple information in a table, following a route on a map, labelling a picture, and so on. The following example is from the Joint Matriculation Board, which has used this technique extensively in its Test of English (Overseas).

> A cart is the simplest type of wheeled vehicle. The following terms are used in describing the parts of one type of cart.
>
> Read the definitions and choose 11 suitable words from the list of 16 to label the parts numbered on the figure below. The first one is done for you. Write the labels on the table below the figure.
>
> axle: a horizontal arm on which wheels turn.
>
> dirtboard: a curved plate of wood or metal projecting from the beam to which the axle is fixed; protects the space between the end of the axle and the hub of the wheel.
>
> exbed: a beam running the width of the cart to which the axle is fixed.
>
> felloe: a section of the wooden rim on the wheel of the cart.
>
> forehead: a plank forming the upper portion of the front end of a cart; usually with a curved top.
>
> longboard: a plank of wood running parallel to the cart sides to form the floor of the cart.

rail: a plank running across the front or back end of a cart.

rave: a horizontal beam forming part of the side wall of the cart.

shaft: one of a pair of wooden boards between which the horse is harnessed to pull the cart.

shutter: a piece of stout wood stretching across the bottom of a cart; joins the sides and supports the floorboards.

sole: a short extension of the lower timbers of the cart frame which projects behind the cart on each side.

standard: a vertical bar of wood which is part of the frame for the side of the cart.

stock: a hub made of elm wood into which wooden bars or spokes are fixed.

strake: an iron tyre made in sections and nailed to the rim of wheel to protect it.

strouter: a curved wooden support to strengthen the cart sides; often elegantly carved.

topboard: a board with a curved top nailed to the top rave of the cart.

A CART

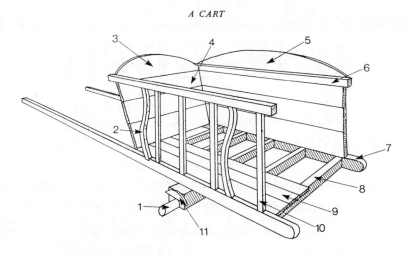

1	axle	7	
2		8	
3		9	
4		10	
5		11	
6			

TECHNIQUES FOR PARTICULAR PURPOSES

Identifying order of events, topics, or arguments   The candidate can be required to number the events etc. as follows in an example taken from the RSA:

In what order does the writer do the following in her article? To answer this, put the number 1 in the answer column next to the one that appears first, and so on. If an idea does not appear in the article, write N/A (not applicable) in the answer column.

a) She gives some of the history of migraine. ☐

b) She recommends specific drugs. ☐

c) She recommends a herbal cure. ☐

d) She describes migraine attacks. ☐

e) She gives general advice to migraine sufferers. ☐

═══ *SUNDAY PLUS* ═══

ONE-SIDED HEADACHE

SUE LIMB begins an occasional series by sufferers from particular ailments

MIGRAINE first visited me when I was 20, and for years afterwards it hung about my life like a blackmailer, only kept at bay by constant sacrifices on my part. Its tyranny was considerable. Many innocent everyday experiences would trigger an attack: stuffy rooms, fluorescent light, minute amounts of alcohol, staying up late, lying in at the weekend, having to wait for meals, loud noises, smoke-filled rooms, the sun, and watching TV for more than two hours.

Work, social life and holidays were all equally disrupted. Naturally, all these prohibitions made me very tense and angry, but anger and tension we~~re~~ dangerous luxuries to a wom~~an~~ with my volatile chemistry.

At its worst, migraine w~~as~~ incapacitating me three time~~s a~~ week, for hours on end. I w~~as~~ losing more than half my life. ~~I~~ had to change my life-sty~~le~~ radically — giving up my j~~ob~~

nd becoming self-employed—
efore the headaches would
etreat. Nowadays, I can
ometimes go for 3 or 4 months
vithout an attack, as long as I
keep my immediate environ-
nent as cool, dark and peaceful
s possible. Sometimes I think
should live in a cave, or lurk
under a stone like a toad.

Migraine is rather like a
ossessive parent or lover who
annot bear to see its victim
njoying ordinary life. Indeed,
ny loved ones have sometimes
n their turn felt jealous at the
vay in which migraine sweeps
ne off my feet and away from
ll company, keeping me in a
larkened room where it feasts
ff me for days on end.

❯ Tyrant, blackmailer, kidnapper, ❯ bore

Migraine sufferers often feel a
eep sense of guilt, for migraine
a bore as well as a tyrant and
idnapper. It destroys social
lans and devastates work-
chedules. Despite its destruc-
ive power, however, the
gnorant still dismiss it as the
roduct of a fevered (and
robably female) imagination:
bit like the vapours. But if
ou've ever felt it, or seen
meone live through it, you
now: migraine is the hardest,
lackest and most terrifying of
veryday pains.

Eyes shrink to the size of
urrants, the face turns deathly
ale, the tongue feels like an old
ardening glove, the entire
ody seems to age about 70
ears, so only a palsied shuffle
the bathroom is possible.
aylight is agonising, a thirst
ges, and the vomiting comes
most as a relief, since in the
aroxysm of nausea the pain
cedes for a few blissful
conds. Above all, the constant

feeling of a dagger striking
through the eyeball and twist-
ing into the brain can make the
sufferer long for death. When
at last (sometimes three days
later) the pain begins to ebb,
and one can slowly creep back
into life, it's like being reborn.

Migraine is the focus of many
myths. It is emphatically not a
recent ailment, or a response to
the stresses of modern life. It
has been with us always. Its
very name derives from the
ancient Greek for *half the skull*
— migraine is always a one-
sided headache. The Egyptians
had a god for it: no doubt he
was more often cursed than

hymned. Some suggest that
migraine sufferers are intellectual types, or particularly
conscientious personalities.
There is little basis for any of
this. Migraine affects 7 to 18
per cent of the population,
impartially; the eggheads and
the emptyheaded alike.

Anxiety, of course, can cause
migraine. And fear of an attack
can itself be a cause of massive
anxiety. Caught in this Catch 22
situation, some sufferers no
longer dare to make any plans,
so reluctant are they to let down
their family or friends yet
again. This incapacitating fear

Sue Limb : ' I was losing more than half my life.'

(Mellontophobia) shows the far-reaching damage migraine is doing to the lives of six million adults in Great Britain alone.

The best thing these sufferers can do is to join the British Migraine Association without delay. This excellent, lively and informal organisation produces leaflets and a newsletter, and organises fund-raising activities to sponsor research. It keeps its members informed about the latest sophisticated drugs available, and also (most importantly) swaps members' hints about herbal treatment and self-help techniques.

There are several drugs available on prescription for the control of migraine, but perhaps the most exciting recent development in research involves a modest hedgerow plant, native to the British Isles and used for centuries by wise women and herbalists for a variety of ailments. It is feverfew (Chrysanthemum Parthenium).

In 1979, Dr E. Stewart Johnson, Research Director of the City of London Migraine Clinic, saw three patients who had been using feverfew as a preventative, and soon afterwards he became involved in its clinical trials. Dr Johnson's work is still progressing, but early results hint at spectacular success. 70 per cent of subjects claim their attacks are less frequent and not so severe : 33 per cent seem completely migraine-free. A few experience unpleasant side-effects (mostly mouth-ulcers : feverfew is a very bitter herb), and it is not recommended for pregnant women. But for the rest of us, three vile-tasting feverfew leaves a day have become indispensable.

Ten years ago I was taking Librium to reduce stress and Ergotamine to treat the actual migraine pain. They were powerful drugs, which left me feeling doped and poisoned, and they didn't always cure the headache, either. Nowadays, I eat my three leaves, feel good, and probably never get the headache in the first place.

Acupuncture has also helped, partly by improving my general sense of well-being, but during a migraine the pain can be immediately dulled and eventually dispersed by needles placed on special points in the feet or temples. Finger pressure on these points can help too, in the absence of an acupuncturist. Locally applied heat (a hot water bottle or acupuncturist moxa stick—a bit like a cigar—is very soothing.

But above all the best thing I've done about my migraine learn to relax all the muscl surrounding the eye. Th natural response to severe pa is to tense up the muscle making the pain worse. Del berately relaxing these muscl instead is a demanding disc pline and requires undisturbe concentration, but the effect dramatic. Immediately the pa becomes less acute.

Migraine is a formidab adversary : tyrant, blackmaile kidnapper, bore ; but aft many years' struggle I real feel I've got it on the run. An though I'm a great admirer the best of Western orthode medicine, it's pleasing that m migraines have finally started slink away when faced not wit a futuristic superpill, but wit the gentle healing practices the East and the Past.

The British Migraine Associatio 178a High Road, Byfleet, We bridge, Surrey KT14 7ED. Te Byfleet 52468.
The City of London Migraine Clin 22 Charterhouse Square, Londo EC1M 6DX will treat suffere caught away from home with a sve attack.

(Limb 1983)

Guessing is possible here, but the probabilities are lower than with straightforward multiple choice.

Identifying referents   One of the 'micro-skills' listed above was the ability to identify referents. An example of an item to test this (based on the original passage about smoking, above) is:

What does the word 'it' (line 25) refer to? ....

Care has to be taken that the precise referent is to be found in the text. It may be necessary on occasion to change the text slightly for this condition to be met.

Guessing the meaning of unfamiliar words from context   This is another of the micro-skills mentioned above. Items may take the form:

Find a single word in the passage (between lines 1 and 25) which has the same meaning as 'making of laws'. (The word in the passage may have an ending like -s, -ing, -ed etc.)

This item also relates to the smoking passage.

An examination of the use of techniques for testing what we have called micro-skills reveals that candidates always need more than the particular micro-skill in order to find the correct response. In order to 'guess the meaning of a word from its context', the context itself has to be understood. The same will normally be true when a referent has to be identified. It is for this reason that it was suggested above that items of this kind have a place in final achievement and proficiency tests.

Relatively few techniques have been presented in this section. This is because, in my view, few basic techniques are needed, and non-professional testers will benefit from concentrating on developing their skills within a limited range, always allowing for the possibility of modifying these techniques for particular purposes and in particular circumstances. Many professional testers appear to have got by with just one – multiple choice! The more usual varieties of cloze and the C-Test technique have been omitted because, while they obviously involve reading to quite a high degree, it is not clear that reading ability is all that they measure. This makes it all the harder to interpret scores on such tests in terms of criterial levels of performance.

WHICH LANGUAGE FOR ITEMS AND RESPONSES?

The wording of reading test items is not meant to cause candidates any difficulties of comprehension. It should always be well within their capabilities, less demanding than the text itself. In the same way, responses should make minimal demands on writing ability. Where candidates share a single native language, this can be used both for items and for responses. There is a danger, however, that items may provide some candidates with more information about the content of the text than they would have obtained from items in the foreign language.

PROCEDURES FOR WRITING ITEMS

The starting point for writing items is a careful reading of the text, having the specified operations in mind. Where relevant, a note should be taken of main points, interesting pieces of information, stages of argument, examples, and so on. The next step is to determine what tasks it is reasonable to expect candidates to be able to perform in relation to these. It is then that draft items can be written. Paragraph numbers and line numbers should be added to the text if items need to make reference to these. The text and items should be presented to colleagues for moderation. Items and even the text may need modification. Only when the test-writing team is satisfied with all the items (from the point of view of reliable candidate performance and reliable scoring) should they be included as part of the test (for pretesting where this is possible).

PRACTICAL ADVICE ON ITEM WRITING

1. In a scanning test, present items in the order in which the answers can be found in the text. Not to do this introduces too much random variation and so lowers the test's reliability.
2. Do not write items for which the correct response can be found without understanding the text (unless that is an ability that you are testing!). Such items usually involve simply matching a string of words in the question with the same string in the text. Thus (around line 45 in the smoking passage, above):

    > What body said that concern over passive smoking had arisen in part through better insulation and draught proofing?

    Better might be:

    > What body has claimed that worries about passive smoking are partly due to improvements in buildings?

    Items that demand simple arithmetic can be useful here. We may learn in one sentence that before 1985 there had only been three hospital operations of a particular kind; in another sentence, that there have been 85 since. An item can ask how many such operations there have been to date, according to the article.
3. Do not include items that some candidates are likely to be able to answer without reading the text. For example:

    > Inhaling smoke from other people's cigarettes can cause ....

    It is not necessary, however, to choose such esoteric topics as has characterised the Joint Matriculation Board's Test in English (Overseas). These have included coracles, the Ruen, and the people of Willington.

A note on scoring

General advice on obtaining reliable scoring has already been given in Chapter 5. It is worth adding here, however, that in a reading test (or a listening test), errors of grammar, spelling or punctuation should not be penalised, provided that it is clear that the candidate has successfully performed the reading task which the item set. The function of a reading test is to test reading ability. To test productive skills at the same time (which is what happens when grammar etc. are taken into account) simply makes the measurement of reading ability less accurate.

READER ACTIVITIES

1. Following the procedures and advice given in the chapter, construct a 12-item reading subtest based on the passage about New Zealand Youth Hostels on page 132. (The passage was used in the Oxford Examination in English as a Foreign Language, Preliminary Level, in 1987.) For each item, make a note of the skill(s) (including micro-skills) you believe it is testing. If possible, have colleagues take the test and provide critical comment. Try to improve the test. Again if possible, administer the test to an appropriate group of students. Score the tests. Interview a few students as to how they arrived at correct responses. Did they use the particular micro-skills that you predicted they would?
2. Compare your questions with the ones to be found in Appendix 2. Can you explain the differences in content and technique? Are there any items which you might want to change? Why? How?
3. The following is part of an exercise designed to help students learn to cope with 'complicated sentences'. How successful would this form of exercise be as part of a reading test? What precisely would it test? Would you want to change the exercise in any way? If so, why and how? Could you make it non-multiple choice? If so, how?

> The intention of other people concerned, such as the Minister of Defence, to influence the government leaders to adapt their policy to fit in with the demands of the right wing, cannot be ignored.
>
> What is the subject of 'cannot be ignored'?
>   a.   the intention
>   b.   other people concerned
>   c.   the Minister of Defence
>   d.   the demands of the right wing.
>
> (Swan 1975)

NEW ZEALAND YOUTH HOSTELS

Where in New Zealand could you find a night's accommodation for only $10 NZ, and share dinner with a friendly crowd from around the world?

In any one of New Zealand's 60 plus youth hostels!

Meeting people is a highlight of any trip, and the communal hostel atmosphere is just the place to meet with fellow travellers. On a typical night you'll find Australians, Canadians, British, Americans, Germans, Danes, and Japanese, and, of course, some New Zealanders at a hostel. Many are making the trip of a lifetime after study, while others are on their third or fourth holiday in New Zealand.

Still others, like Don and Jean Cameron from South Australia, are on a "retirement" holiday, three months motorcycling the South Island. I met up with Don and Jean last summer at the Queenstown hostel. "Our friends thought we were mad" laughed Jean, "but we find the hostels very comfortable, and we've met so many interesting people that we'll have to make a world trip next year just to see them all!"

SPECTACULAR

The Queenstown hostel is tucked onto the shoreline of Lake Wakatipu, with spectacular views across to the rugged Remarkable Mountains. This busy tourist town is the centre for both leisurely and adventurous activities – from a cruise on the historic steamer Earnslaw and visit to a working sheep-station, to fast and furious white water rafting on the Kawarau and Shotover Rivers.

Further north, at Mt Cook, the Youth Hostel Association's biggest ever project is under way. The present hostel, usually bulging at the seams, is being replaced with a large specially designed hostel, which will soon be opening.

As New Zealand's tallest mountain, Mt Cook is a major tourist attraction, but you don't need to be a climber to enjoy the park. Rangers can suggest a wide range of walks that open up the alpine world – massive glacier moraines, icy streams, and tiny alpine plants.

WAFFLES

Across the Southern Alps, Westland National Park offers a quite different experience. The Franz Josef and Fox glaciers, centre-pieces of this spectacular area, plunge down from the main divide through Westland's luxuriant forest to only a few hundred metres above sea level.

A short car ride from the Franz Josef glacier is one of New Zealand's nicest hostels. The manager is renowned for cooking up the best ever waffles and ice cream as an after-dinner treat. They're guaranteed to put back the calories you took off walking up to the glacier lookout, or on a forest or lakeside ramble.

The South Island mountains and lakes are a favourite of mine, but whatever your holiday plans you'll find youth hostels there. Prefer a lazy-beach stay with sun-bathing, swimming, sailing, or scuba diving? With a coastline of 10,000 km, the choice is yours!

The Bay of Islands (north of Auckland) has long been a mecca for all of the sea sports. Two hostels serve the Bay – one at the historic township of Kerikeri, the other on the Whangaroa Harbour. A boat charter company offers Kerikeri hostellers a special discount – a whole day out on a sailing boat for around $30 NZ per person.

Whangaroa's sheltered harbour, sub-tropical bush, and a comfortable hostel with superb harbour views make for a perfect break. After a lazy day on a cruise and trying our hand at fishing, a group of us headed down to the local hotel for a freshly caught seafood dinner – some of the ones that didn't get away.

If the world of bubbling hot pools and soaring geysers is more your scene, then a stop in Rotorua is a must. The Rotorua hostel is right in the middle of town, just an easy walk to Whakarewarewa Thermal Reserve and the hot pools. For longer trips hire a bicycle from the hostel, or use any of the wide range of bus tours to see the area.

The hostel network hasn't forgotten the major cities. Auckland has an inner-city and a suburban hostel, as well as two island hideaways. Wellington, the capital and transport centre of the country, has an inner city hostel; while Christchurch boasts a stately home hostel as well as a downtown base. Dunedin, the Scottish city of the south, has one of the grandest of all – with small bedrooms and three living rooms.

Whether you're in New Zealand for a short stop-over, or here for several months, hostels will stretch your travel funds much further. Hostels aren't luxury hotels, but they do provide simple, comfortable accommodation with good kitchen, laundry and bathroom facilities. Kitchens are well equipped, all you need supply is the food. Many hostels have a small shop too, selling meal-sized portions of food.

For further information about New Zealand youth hostels, write to Youth Hostel Association National Office, PO Box 436, Christchurch, New Zealand.

4. The following exercise is meant to improve the learner's ability to 'develop a mental schema of a text'. Subject it to the same considerations as the previous exercise type.

B I told you a bit of a lie

Reading comprehension; vocabulary;
grammar (conditionals).

1 Read the text. Don't take more than five
minutes. You can use a dictionary or ask the
teacher for help (but try to guess the meaning
of a word first).

clearing up crimes like petty
theft and burglary.

Parachutist, 81, wins place of honour at jump

Even experts were a little surprised when a man of 62 turned up at a parachute training school and said he was interested in learning to become a parachutist.

They agreed to put him through the course, but only after giving him a series of tests to prove that he was fit enough.

Mr Archie Macfarlane completed the course successfully, surprising everyone with his agility and toughness.

A few weeks later, when he was ready for his first jump, he confessed to the chief instructor: "I told you a bit of a lie. I'm really 75."

That was six years ago and yesterday Archie Macfarlane made his 18th jump. He was given the place of honour – first out of the plane – at a weekend meeting for parachutists over 40 years old.

Archie's interest in parachuting is just one of the hobbies that his wife has to worry about. He also enjoys motorcycling and mountaineering.

Last year he fell while climbing on Snowdon, and had to be rescued by helicopter.

His daughter said: "Sometimes I think he ought to give it all up. But as my mother says, so long as he's happy, it's better than being miserable. He tried hang-gliding once and said he thought it was a bit too easy."

Now Archie is thinking of taking up water-skiing.

(adapted from a press report)

2 Here are three summaries of the text. Which do you think is the best?

1. Archie Macfarlane started parachuting when
he was 75, and he has done 18 parachute jumps
over the last six years. Recently he was given
the place of honour at a parachutists' meeting.
When he started parachuting, he told a lie
about his age. His wife and daughter are
worried about him.

2. Archie Macfarlane is an unusual person.
Although he is an old man, he is interested in
very tough sporting activities like parachuting,
mountaineering and water-skiing. His wife and
daughter are worried, but think it's best for him
to do things that make him happy.

3. When Archie Macfarlane first learnt parachute
jumping, he pretended that he was only 62. In
fact, he is much older than that, and he is really
becoming too old to take part in outdoor
sporting activities. His wife and daughter wish
that he would stop motorcycling,
mountaineering and hang-gliding.

(Swan and Walter 1988)

Further reading

Shohamy (1984) reports on research that explored the effect of writing
items in the candidates' native language.

12 Testing listening

It may seem rather odd to test listening separately from speaking, since the two skills are typically exercised together in oral interaction. However, there are occasions, such as listening to the radio, listening to lectures, or listening to railway station announcements, when no speaking is called for. Also, as far as testing is concerned, there may be situations where the testing of oral ability is considered, for one reason or another, impractical, but where a test of listening is included for its backwash effect on the development of oral skills.

Because it is a receptive skill, the testing of listening parallels in most ways the testing of reading. This chapter will therefore spend little time on issues common to the testing of the two skills and will concentrate more on matters which are particular to listening. The reader who plans to construct a listening test is advised to read both this and the previous chapter.

The special problems in constructing listening tests arise out of the transient nature of the spoken language. Listeners cannot usually move backwards and forwards over what is being said in the way that they can a written text. The one apparent exception to this, when a tape-recording is put at the listener's disposal, does not represent a typical listening task for most people. Ways of dealing with these problems are discussed later in the chapter.

Specifying what the candidate should be able to do

Content

OPERATIONS

As with reading, these may be at more than one level of analysis:

Macro-skills would be directly related to candidates' needs or to course objectives, and might include:

— listening for specific information
— obtaining gist of what is being said
— following directions
— following instructions

Microskills might include:

- interpretation of intonation patterns (recognition of sarcasm, etc.)
- recognition of function of structures (such as interrogative as request, for example, Could you pass the salt?)

At the lowest level are abilities like being able to distinguish between phonemes (for example between /w/ and /v/).

It seems to me that abilities at the lowest level are only of interest for diagnostic purposes, and the relevant information can be readily obtained through informal means.

TYPES OF TEXT

These might be first specified as monologue, dialogue, or multi-participant; and further specified: announcement, talk or lecture, instructions, directions, etc.

ADDRESSEES

Texts may be intended for the general public, students (either specialists or generalists), young children, and so on.

TOPICS

These will often be indicated in quite general terms.

Setting criterial levels of performance

If the test is set at an appropriate level, then, as with reading, a near perfect set of responses may be required for a 'pass'.

Setting the tasks

Selecting samples of speech

Passages must be chosen with the test specifications in mind. If we are interested in how candidates can cope with language intended for native speakers, then ideally we should use samples of authentic speech. In fact these can usually be readily found, with a little effort. Possible sources are: radio broadcasts, teaching materials (see the *Further reading* section for examples), and our own recordings of native speakers. If, on the other hand, we want to know whether candidates can understand language which may be addressed to them as non-native speakers, these too can be obtained from teaching materials and recordings of native speakers which we can make ourselves. In some cases the indifferent quality of the recording may necessitate re-recording. It seems to me, though not everyone would agree, that a poor recording introduces difficulties

135

F

additional to the ones that we want to set, and so reduces the validity of the test. It may also introduce unreliability, since the performance of individuals may be affected by the recording faults in different degrees from occasion to occasion. In some cases (see below), a recording may be used simply as the basis for a 'live' presentation.

If the quality of a recording is unsatisfactory, it is always possible to make a transcription and then re-record it. Similarly, if details of what is said on the recording interfere with the writing of good items, testers should feel able to edit the recording, or to make a fresh recording from the amended transcript.

If recordings are made especially for the test, then care must be taken to make them as natural as possible. There is typically a fair amount of redundancy in spoken language: people are likely to paraphrase what they have already said ('What I mean to say is ... '), and to remove this redundancy is to make the listening task unnatural. In particular, we should avoid passages originally intended for reading, like the following, which appeared as an example of a listening comprehension passage for a well-known test:

> She found herself in a corridor which was unfamiliar, but after trying one or two doors discovered her way back to the stone-flagged hall which opened onto the balcony. She listened for sounds of pursuit but heard none. The hall was spacious, devoid of decoration: no flowers, no pictures.

This is an extreme example, but test writers should be wary of trying to create spoken English out of their imagination: it is better to base the passage on a genuine recording, or a transcript of one.

Suitable passages may be of various lengths, depending on what is being tested. A passage lasting ten minutes or more might be needed to test the ability to follow an academic lecture, while twenty seconds could be sufficient to give a set of directions.

Writing items

For extended listening, such as a lecture, a useful first step is to listen to the passage and take notes, putting down what it is that candidates should be able to get from the passage. We can then attempt to write items that check whether or not they have got what they should be able to get. This note-making procedure will not normally be necessary for shorter passages, which will have been chosen (or constructed) to test particular abilities.

In testing extended listening, it is essential to keep items sufficiently far apart in the passage. If two items are close to each other, candidates may miss the second of them through no fault of their own, and the effect of this on subsequent items can be disastrous (candidates listening for 'answers' that have already passed). Since a single faulty item can have such an effect, it is particularly important to trial extended listening tests, even if only on colleagues aware of the potential problems.

Candidates should be warned by key words that appear both in the item and in the passage that the information called for is about to be heard. For example, an item may ask about *'the second point that the speaker makes'* and candidates will hear *'My second point is ...'*. The wording does not have to be identical, but candidates should be given fair warning in the passage. It would be wrong, for instance, to ask about *'what the speaker regards as her most important point'* when the speaker makes the point and only afterwards refers to it as the most important. This is an extreme example; less obvious cases should be revealed through trialling.

Other than in exceptional circumstances (such as when the candidates are required to take notes on a lecture without knowing what the items will be, see below), candidates should be given sufficient time at the outset to familiarise themselves with the items.

As was suggested for reading in the previous chapter, there seems no sound reason not to write items and accept responses in the native language of the candidates. This will in fact often be what would happen in the real world, when a fellow native speaker asks for information that we have to listen for in the foreign language.

POSSIBLE TECHNIQUES

Multiple choice   The advantages and disadvantages of using multiple choice in extended listening tests are similar to those identified for reading tests in the previous chapter. In addition, however, there is the problem of the candidates having to hold in their heads four or more alternatives while listening to the passage and, after responding to one item, of taking in and retaining the alternatives for the next item. If multiple choice is to be used, then the alternatives must be kept short and simple. The alternatives in the following, which appeared in a sample listening test of a well-known examination, are probably too complex.

> When stopped by the police, how is the motorist advised to behave?
> A He should say nothing until he has seen his lawyer.
> B He should give only what additional information the law requires.
> C He should say only what the law requires.
> D He should in no circumstances say anything.

Short answer   Provided that the items themselves are brief, and only really short responses are called for, short-answer items can work well in listening tests. The completion variety, requiring minimal writing from the candidate, is particularly useful.

Information transfer This technique is as useful in testing listening as it is in testing reading, since it makes minimal demands on productive skills. It can involve such activities as the labelling of diagrams or pictures, completing forms, or showing routes on a map. The following example, which is taken from the ARELS examination, is one of a series of related tasks in which the candidate 'visits' a friend who has been involved in a motor accident. The friend has hurt his hand, and the candidate (listening to a tape-recording) has to help Tom write his report of the accident. Time allowed for each piece of writing is indicated.

> In this question you must write your answers. Tom also has to draw a sketch map of the accident. He has drawn the streets, but he can't write in the names. He asks you to fill in the details. Look at the sketch map in your book. Listen to Tom and write on the map what he tells you.

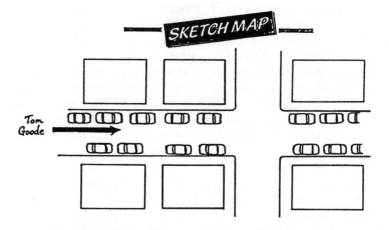

Tom: This is a rough map of where the accident happened. There's the main road going across with the cars parked on both sides of it – that's Queen Street. You'd better write the name on it – Queen Street. (*five seconds*) And the smaller road going across it is called Green Road. Write Green Road on the smaller road. (*five seconds*) Now, I was riding along Queen Street where the arrow is and the little boy ran into the road from my right, from between the two buildings on the right. The building on the corner is the Star Cinema – just write Star on the corner building. (*five seconds*) And the one next to it is the Post Office. Write P.O. on that building next to the cinema. (*five seconds*) Well the boy ran out between those two buildings, and into the road. Can you put an arrow in where the boy came from, like I did for me and the bike, but for the boy? (*five seconds*) When he ran out I turned left away from him and hit one of the parked cars. It was the second car back from the crossroads on the left. Put a cross on the second car back. (*three seconds*) It was quite funny really. It was parked right outside the police station. A policeman heard the bang and came out at once. You'd better write Police on the police station there on the corner. (*five seconds*) I think that's all we need. Thanks very much.

Note taking   Where the ability to take notes while listening to, say, a lecture is in question, this activity can be quite realistically replicated in the testing situation. Candidates take notes during the talk, and only after the talk is finished do they see the items to which they have to respond. When constructing such a test, it is essential to use a passage from which notes *can* be taken successfully. This will only become clear when the task is first attempted by test writers.

It should go without saying that, since this is a testing task which might otherwise be unfamiliar, potential candidates should be made aware of its existence and, if possible, be provided with practice materials. If this is not done, then the performance of many candidates will lead us to underestimate their ability.

Partial dictation   While partial dictation (see Chapter 8) may not be a particularly authentic listening activity (though in lectures at university, for instance, there is a certain amount of dictation), it can be useful. It may be possible to administer a partial dictation when no other test of listening is practical. It can also be used diagnostically to test students' ability to cope with particular difficulties (such as weak forms in English).

Recordings or live presentations?   The great advantage of using recordings when administering a listening test is that there is uniformity in what is presented to the candidates. This is fine if the recording is to be listened to in a well-maintained language laboratory or in a room with good acoustic qualities and with suitable equipment (the recording should be equally clear in all parts of the room). If these conditions do not obtain, then a live presentation is to be preferred.

If presentations are to be live, then greatest uniformity (and so reliability) will be achieved if there is just a single speaker for each (part of a) test. If the test is being administered at the same time in a number of rooms, more than one speaker will be called for. In either case, a recording should be made of the presentation, with which speakers can be trained, so that the intended emphases, timing etc. will be observed with consistency. Needless to say, speakers should have a good command of the language of the test and be generally highly reliable, responsible, and trustworthy individuals.

Scoring the listening test

It is probably worth mentioning again that in scoring a test of a receptive skill there is no reason to deduct points for errors of grammar or spelling, provided that it is clear that the correct response was intended.

1. Choose an extended recording of spoken language that would be appropriate for a group of students with whom you are familiar (you may get this from published materials, or you may record a native speaker or something on the radio). Play a five-minute stretch to yourself and take notes. On the basis of the notes, construct eight short-answer items. Ask colleagues to take the test and comment on it. Amend the test as necessary, and administer it to the group of students you had in mind, if possible. Analyse the results. Go through the test item by item with the students and ask for their comments. How far, and how well, is each item testing what you thought it would test?

2. Design short items that attempt to discover whether candidates can recognise: sarcasm, surprise, boredom, elation. Try these on colleagues and students as above.

3. Design a test that requires candidates to draw (or complete) simple pictures. Decide exactly what the test is measuring. Think what other things could be measured using this or similar techniques. Administer the test and see if the students agree with you about what is being measured.

Further reading

Examples of recordings in English that might be used as the basis of listening tests are Crystal and Davy (1975); Hughes and Trudgill (1987), if regional British accents are relevant.

13   Testing grammar and vocabulary

Testing grammar

Why test grammar?

Can one justify the separate testing of grammar? There was a time when this would have seemed a very odd question. Control of grammatical structures was seen as the very core of language ability and it would have been unthinkable not to test it. But times have changed. As far as proficiency tests are concerned, there has been a shift towards the view that since it is language *skills* that are usually of interest, then it is these which should be tested directly, not the abilities that seem to underlie them. For one thing, it is argued, there is more to any skill than the sum of its parts; one cannot accurately predict mastery of the skill by measuring control of what we believe to be the abilities that underlie it. For another, as has been argued earlier in this book, the backwash effect of tests which measure mastery of skills directly may be thought preferable to that of tests which might encourage the learning of grammatical structures in isolation, with no apparent need to *use* them. Considerations of this kind have resulted in the absence of any grammar component in some well-known proficiency tests.

But most proficiency tests which are administered on a large scale still retain a grammar section. One reason for this must be the ease with which large numbers of items can be administered and scored within a short period of time. Related to that, and at least as important, is the question of content validity. If we decide to test writing ability directly, then we are severely limited in the number of topics, styles of writing, and what we earlier referred to as 'operations', that we can cover in any one version of the test. We cannot be completely confident that the sample chosen is truly representative of all possibilities. Neither can we be sure, of course, that a (proficiency) grammar test includes a good sample of all possible grammatical elements. But the very fact that there can be so many items does put the grammar test at an advantage.

Even if one has doubts about testing grammar in a proficiency test, there is often good cause to include a grammar component in the achievement, placement and diagnostic tests of teaching institutions. It seems unlikely that there are many institutions, however 'communicative' their approach, that do not teach some grammar in some guise or other. Wherever the teaching of grammar is thought necessary, then consideration should be given to the advisability of including a grammar component in achievement tests. If this is done, however, it would seem prudent, from the point of view of backwash, not to give such components too much prominence in relation to tests of skills, the development of which will normally constitute the primary objectives of language courses.

Whether or not grammar has an important place in an institution's teaching, it has to be accepted that grammatical ability, or rather the lack of it, sets limits to what can be achieved in the way of skills performance. The successful writing of academic assignments, for example, must depend to some extent on command of more than the most elementary grammatical structures. It would seem to follow from this that in order to place students in the most appropriate class for the development of such skills, knowledge of a student's grammatical ability would be very useful information. There appears to be room for a grammar component in at least some placement tests.

It would be particularly useful to know for individual students (and for groups of students) what gaps exist in their grammatical repertoire. Unfortunately, as explained in Chapter 3, for the moment at least, to obtain *reliable* and more than rudimentary diagnostic information of this kind would involve the development and administration of long and unwieldy tests. Computer-based testing may bring progress in this field in the near future.

WRITING SPECIFICATIONS

For achievement tests where teaching objectives or the syllabus list the grammatical structures to be taught, specification of content should be quite straightforward. When there is no such listing it becomes necessary to infer from textbooks and other teaching materials what structures are being taught. Specifications for a placement test will normally include *all* of the structures identified in this way, as well as, perhaps, those structures the command of which is taken for granted in even the lowest classes.

SAMPLING

This will reflect an attempt to give the test content validity by selecting widely from the structures specified. It should also take account of what are regarded for one reason or another as the most important structures. It should *not* deliberately concentrate on the structures which happen to be easiest to test.

WRITING ITEMS

Many, if not most, language testing handbooks encourage the testing of grammar by means of multiple choice items, often to the exclusion of just about any other method. Chapter 8 of this book gave a number of reasons why testing within institutions should *avoid* excessive use of multiple choice. In this section, there will be no examples of multiple choice items. Though all the techniques can be given a multiple choice format, the reader who attempts to write such items can often expect to have problems in finding suitable distractors.

The techniques to be presented here are just three in number: paraphrase, completion, and modified cloze. Used with imagination, these should prove sufficient for most grammar testing purposes. They have in common what should be appreciated as a highly desirable quality: they require the student to supply grammatical structures appropriately and not simply to recognise their correct use. Ways of scoring are suggested in the next section.

PARAPHRASE

These require the student to write a sentence equivalent in meaning to one that is given. It is helpful to give part of the paraphrase in order to restrict the students to the grammatical structure being tested. Thus:

1. Testing passive, past continuous form.

> When we arrived, a policeman was questioning the bank clerk.
> When we arrived, the bank clerk ....

2. Testing present perfect with *for*.

> It is six years since I last saw him.
> I .... six years.

COMPLETION

This technique can be used to test a variety of structures. Note how the context in a passage like the following, from the Cambridge First Certificate in English *Testpack 1*, allows the tester to elicit specific structures, in this case interrogative forms.

In the following conversation, the sentences numbered (1) to (6) have been left incomplete. Complete them suitably. Read the whole conversation before you begin to answer the question.

(Mr Cole wants a job in Mr Gilbert's export business. He has come for an interview.)

Mr Gilbert: Good morning, Mr Cole. Please come in and sit down. Now let me see. (1) Which school ....?

G

Testing grammar and vocabulary

Mr Cole:	Whitestone College.
Mr Gilbert:	(2) And when ....?
Mr Cole:	In 1972, at the end of the summer term.
Mr Gilbert:	(3) And since then what ....?
Mr Cole:	I worked in a bank for a year. Then I took my present job, selling cars. But I would like a change now.
Mr Gilbert:	(4) Well, what sort of a job ....?
Mr Cole:	I'd really like to work in your Export Department.
Mr Gilbert:	That might be a little difficult. What are your qualifications? (5) I mean what languages .... besides English?
Mr Cole:	Well, only a little French.
Mr Gilbert:	That would be a big disadvantage, Mr Cole. (6) Could you tell me why ....?
Mr Cole:	Because I'd like to travel and to meet people from other countries.
Mr Gilbert:	I don't think I can help you at present, Mr Cole. Perhaps you ought to try a travel agency.

MODIFIED CLOZE

Testing prepositions of place

John looked round the room. The book was still .... the table. The cat was .... the chair. He wondered what was .... the box .... the telephone.

And so on.

144

Testing articles
(Candidates are required to write *the, a* or *NA* – No Article.)

> In England children go to .... school from Monday to Friday.
> .... school that Mary goes to is very small. She walks there each
> morning with .... friend. One morning they saw ....
> man throwing .... stones and .... pieces of wood at
> .... dog. .... dog was afraid of .... man.

And so on.

Testing a variety of grammatical structures
(The text is taken from Colin Dexter *The Secret of Annexe 3*.)

> When the old man died, ... was probably no great joy
> .... heaven; and quite certainly little if any real grief in
> Charlbury Drive, the pleasantly unpretentious cul-de-sac ....
> semi-detached houses to which he .... retired.

Testing sentence linking
(A one-word answer is required.)

> The council must do something to improve transport in the city.
> ...., they will lose the next election.

SCORING PRODUCTION GRAMMAR TESTS

The important thing is to be clear about what each item is testing, and to award points for that only. There may be just one element, such as the definite article, and all available points should be awarded for that; nothing should be deducted for non-grammatical errors, or for errors in grammar which is not being tested by the item. For instance, a candidate should not be penalised for a missing third person -s when the item is testing relative pronouns; *opend* should be accepted for *opened*, without penalty.

If two elements are being tested in an item, then points may be assigned to each of them (for example present perfect form and *since* with past time reference point). Alternatively, it can be stipulated that both elements have to be correct for any points to be awarded, which makes sense in those cases where getting one element wrong means that the student does not have full control of the structure.

For valid and reliable scoring of grammar items of the kind advocated here, careful preparation of the scoring key is necessary. A key for items in the previous section might be along the following lines.

>>>→

Paraphrase
1. Must have *W as being* .... *ed* – 1 point
2. *I haven't* [or *have not*] – 1 point
   seen – 1 point
   for six years – 1 point

Alternatively, all three elements could be required for a point to be given, depending on the information that is being looked for.

Completion The Cambridge First Certificate Testpack, from which the completion items were taken, is rather less explicit than one might wish (though no doubt in an actual examination scorers would be given more detailed instructions). Thus:

> Whole mark for each question formed correctly with auxiliary and inversion (except No. 6 'why you want to' etc.) and with tense suitable to context. Bonus for continuous tense in No. 3. The American phrase 'quit college' for 'leave school' allowed.

Modified cloze As was mentioned in Chapter 8, it is helpful if candidates are required to put their responses in numbered spaces at the right-hand side of the page. Checking against the key is then very straightforward.

Prepositions	Articles
1. on	1. NA
2. under/beneath	2. The
3. in/inside	3. a
4. near/beside	4. a
	5. NA
Various structures	6. NA
1. there	7. a
2. in	8. The
3. of	9. the
4. had	

Sentence linking
otherwise

Testing vocabulary

Why test vocabulary?

Any doubts about the advisability of testing grammar apply equally to the testing of vocabulary. Clearly knowledge of vocabulary is essential to the development and demonstration of linguistic skills. But that does not necessarily mean that it should be tested separately.

Similar reasons may be advanced for testing vocabulary in proficiency tests to those used to support the inclusion of a grammar section (though vocabulary has its special sampling problems). However, the arguments for a separate component in other kinds of test may not have the same strength. One suspects that much less time is devoted to the regular, conscious teaching of vocabulary than to the similar teaching of grammar. If there is little teaching of vocabulary, it may be argued that there is little call for achievement tests of vocabulary. At the same time, it *is* to be hoped that vocabulary *learning* is taking place. Achievement tests that measure the extent of this learning (and encourage it) perhaps do have a part to play in institutional testing. For those who believe that systematic teaching of vocabulary is desirable, vocabulary achievement tests are appreciated for their backwash effect.

The usefulness (and indeed the feasibility) of a general diagnostic test of vocabulary is not readily apparent. As far as placement tests are concerned, we would not normally require, or expect, a particular set of lexical items to be a prerequisite for a particular language class. All we would be looking for is some general indication of the adequacy of the student's vocabulary. The learning of specific lexical items in class will rarely depend on previous knowledge of other, specified items. One alternative is to use a published test of vocabulary. The other is to construct one's own vocabulary proficiency test.

WRITING SPECIFICATIONS

How do we specify the vocabulary for an achievement test? If vocabulary is being consciously taught, then presumably all the items thereby presented to the students should be included in the specifications. To these we can add all the new items that the students have met in other activities (reading, listening, etc.). A subsequent step is to group the items in terms of their relative importance.

We have suggested that a vocabulary placement test will be in essence a proficiency test. The usual way to specify the lexical items that may be tested in a proficiency test is to make reference to one of the published word lists that indicate the *frequency* with which the words have been found to be used (see *Further reading*).

SAMPLING

Words can be grouped according to their frequency and usefulness. From each of these groups items can be taken at random, with more being selected from the groups containing the more frequent and useful words.

ITEM WRITING

Recognition This is one testing problem for which multiple choice can be recommended without too many reservations. For one thing, distractors are usually readily available. For another, there seems unlikely to be any serious harmful backwash effect, since guessing the meaning of vocabulary items is something which we would probably wish to encourage. However, the writing of successful items is not without its difficulties.

Items may involve a number of different operations:

1. Synonyms
Choose the alternative (A,B,C,D) which is closest in meaning to the word on the left of the page.

> *gleam*   A. gather   B. shine   C. welcome   D. clean

The writer of this item has probably chosen the first alternative because of the word *glean*. The fourth may have been chosen because of the similarity of its sound to that of *gleam*. Whether these distractors would work as intended would only be discovered through pretesting.

Note that all of the options are words which the candidates are expected to know. If, for example, *welcome* were replaced by *groyne*, most candidates, recognising that it is the meaning of the stem (gleam) on which they are being tested, would dismiss *groyne* immediately.

On the other hand, the item could have a common word as the stem with four less frequent words as options:

> *shine*   A. malm   B. gleam   C. loam   D. snarl

Note that in both items it is the word *gleam* which is being tested.

2. Definitions

> *loathe* means A. dislike intensely
> B. become seriously ill
> C. search carefully
> D. look very angry

Note that all of the options are of about the same length. It is said that test-takers who are uncertain of which option is correct will tend to choose the one which is noticeably different from the others. If *dislike intensely* is to be used as the definition, then the distractors should be made to resemble it. In this case the item writer has included some notion of intensity in all of the options.

Again the difficult word could be one of the options.

> One word that means to *dislike intensely* is A. growl
> B. screech
> C. sneer
> D. loathe

3. Gap filling (multiple choice)

Context, rather than a definition or a synonym, can be used to test knowledge of a lexical item.

> The strong wind .... the man's efforts to put up the tent.
> A. disabled   C. deranged
> B. hampered   D. regaled

Note that the context should not itself contain words which the candidates are unlikely to know.

PRODUCTION

The testing of vocabulary productively is so difficult that it is practically never attempted in proficiency tests. Information on receptive ability is regarded as sufficient. The suggestions presented below are intended only for possible use in achievement tests.

1. Pictures

The main difficulty in testing productive lexical ability is the need to limit the candidate to the (usually one) lexical item that we have in mind, while using only simple vocabulary ourselves. One way round this is to use pictures.

> Each of the objects drawn below has a letter against it. Write down the names of the objects:
> A ....
> B ....
> C ....
> D ....
> E ....
> F ....

This method of testing vocabulary is obviously restricted to concrete nouns which can be unambiguously drawn.

2. Definitions
This may work for a range of lexical items:

> A .... is a person who looks after our teeth.
> .... is frozen water.
> .... is the second month of the year.

But not all items can be identified uniquely from a definition: any definition of say *feeble* would be unlikely to exclude all of its synonyms. Nor can all words be defined entirely in words more common or simpler than themselves.

3. Gap filling
This can take the form of one or more sentences with a single word missing.

> Because of the snow, the football match was .... until the following week.

> I .... to have to tell you this, Mrs Jones, but your husband has had an accident.

Too often there is an alternative word to the one we have in mind. Indeed the second item above has at least two acceptable responses (which was not intended when it was written!). This problem can be solved by giving the first letter of the word (possibly more) and even an indication of the number of letters.

Postscript

This chapter should end with a reminder that while grammar and vocabulary contribute to communicative skills, they are rarely to be regarded as ends in themselves. It is essential that tests should not accord them too much importance, and so create a backwash effect that undermines the achievement of the objectives of teaching and learning where these are communicative in nature.

READER ACTIVITIES

1. Construct items to test the following:
   Conditional: *If .... had ...., ... would have ....*
   Comparison of equality
   Relative pronoun *whose*
   Past continuous: *.... was -ing, when ....*
   Which of the techniques suggested in the chapter suits each structure best? Can you say why?

2. Produce two vocabulary tests by writing two items for each of the following words, including, if possible, a number of production items. Give each test to a different (but comparable) group of students (you could divide one class into two). Compare performance on the pairs of items. Can differences of performance be attributed to a difference in technique?

beard	sigh	bench	deaf	genial
greedy	mellow	callow	tickle	weep

Further reading

West (1953) is a standard word list.

14   Test administration

The best test may give unreliable and invalid results if it is not well administered. This chapter is intended simply to provide readers with an ordered set of points to bear in mind when administering a test. While most of these points will be very obvious, it is surprising how often some of them can be forgotten without a list of this kind to refer to. Tedious as many of the suggested procedures are, they are important for successful testing. Once established, they become part of a routine which all concerned take for granted.

Preparation

The key to successful test administration is careful advance preparation. In particular, attention should be given to the following:

Materials and equipment

1. Organise the printing of test booklets and answer sheets in plenty of time. Check that there are no errors or any faulty reproduction.
2. If previously used test booklets are to be employed, check that there are no marks (for example underlining) left by candidates.
3. Number all the test materials consecutively; this permits greater security before, during, and after test administration.
4. Check that there are sufficient keys for scorers, and that these are free of error.
5. Check that all equipment (tape-recorders, loud speaker system, etc.) is in good working order in plenty of time for repair or replacement.

Examiners

6. Detailed instructions should be prepared for all examiners. In these, an attempt should be made to cover all eventualities, though the unexpected will always occur. These instructions should be gone through with the examiners at least the day before the test is administered. An indication of possible content can be derived from the *Administration* section, below.

7. Examiners should practise directions which they will have to read out to candidates.
8. Examiners who will have to use equipment (for example tape-recorders) should familiarise themselves with its operation.
9. Examiners who have to read aloud for a listening test should practise, preferably with a model tape-recording (see Chapter 12).
10. Oral examiners must be thoroughly familiar with the test procedures and rating system to be used (only properly trained oral examiners should be involved).

Invigilators (or proctors)

11. Detailed instructions should also be prepared for invigilators, and should be the subject of a meeting with them. See *Administration*, below, for possible content.

Candidates

12. Every candidate should be given full instructions (where to go, at what time, what to bring, what they should do if they arrive late, etc.).
13. There should be an examination number for each candidate.

Rooms

14. Rooms should be chosen which are *quiet*, and *large enough* to accommodate comfortably the intended number of candidates; there should be sufficient space between candidates to prevent copying.
15. For listening tests, the rooms must have satisfactory acoustic qualities.
16. The layout of rooms (placing of desks or tables) should be arranged well in advance.
17. Ideally, in each room there should be a clock visible to all candidates.

Administration

18. Candidates should be required to arrive well before the intended starting time for the test.
19. Candidates arriving late should not be admitted to the room. If it is feasible and thought appropriate, they may be redirected to another room where latecomers (up to a certain time) can be tested. They should certainly not be allowed to disturb the concentration of those already taking the test.

20. The identity of candidates should be checked.
21. If possible, candidates should be seated in such a way as to prevent friends being in a position to pass information to each other.
22. The examiner should give clear instructions to candidates about what they are required to do. These should include information on how they should attract the attention of an invigilator if this proves necessary, and what candidates who finish before time are to do. They should also warn students of the consequences of any irregular behaviour, including cheating, and emphasise the necessity of maintaining silence throughout the duration of the test.
23. Test materials should be distributed to candidates individually by the invigilators in such a way that the position of each test paper and answer sheet is known by its number. A record should be made of these. Candidates should not be allowed to distribute test materials.
24. The examiner should instruct candidates to provide the required details (such as examination number, date) on the answer sheet or test booklet.
25. If spoken test instructions are to be given in addition to those written on the test paper, the examiner should read these, including whatever examples have been agreed upon.
26. It is essential that the examiner time the test precisely, making sure that everyone starts on time and does not continue after time.
27. Once the test is in progress, invigilators should unobtrusively monitor the behaviour of candidates. They will deal with any irregularities in the way laid down in their instructions.
28. During the test, candidates should be allowed to leave the room only one at a time, ideally accompanied by an invigilator.
29. Invigilators should ensure that candidates stop work immediately they are told to do so. Candidates should remain in their places until all the materials have been collected and their numbers checked.

Appendix 1 Statistical analysis of test results

As was indicated in Chapter 7, the point of carrying out pretesting is to be able to analyse performance on the test and thereby identify any weaknesses or problems there may be before the test is administered to the target candidates. Even when pretesting is not possible, it is nevertheless worthwhile to analyse performance on the test after the main administration. Part of the analysis will be simply to provide a summary of how the candidates have done, and to check on the test's reliability and so have some idea of how dependable are the test scores. This chapter will provide the reader with an outline of how such analysis can be conducted. It will make use only of the most elementary arithmetic concepts, which should be well within the abilities of any reader. It will also restrict itself to operations which can be carried out on an inexpensive calculator.[1]

While these deliberate restrictions may make post-test analysis accessible to more readers than would otherwise be the case, it also means that some of the procedures described are rather less sophisticated than one would hope to see applied in ideal circumstances. References to procedures commonly used by professional testers, which will give more dependable results, can be found in the *Further reading* section.

Summarising the scores

The mean

The first step is to calculate the *mean* score (or average score) for each component of the test, as well as for the whole test. The mean is the sum of all the scores divided by the number of scores. Thus the mean of 14, 34, 56, 68 is: $(14 + 34 + 56 + 68) \div 4 = 43$.

If the components of the test have equal weight, then the mean for the whole test will be the mean of the means for each section. Thus if the mean for reading is 40 and the mean for writing is 48, then the mean for the complete test will be 44.

If the components are weighted differently (say reading 45 per cent, listening

---

1. All that is needed is a calculator that gives *square roots* (look for the symbol $\sqrt{}$), *means* (look for the symbol $\bar{x}$), *standard deviations* (look for SD, s, or σ) and *correlations* (look for r). The one apparent exception, the use of a micro-computer to carry out Rasch analysis, is mentioned only as a matter of interest to those readers who might be in a position to benefit from this.

55 per cent), then the easiest thing is to enter the test total scores (which take account of the weighting) into the calculator. Whether or not there is differential weighting, these scores will have to be entered to calculate the standard deviation for the whole test (see below).

The standard deviation

Very different sets of scores may have the same mean. For example, a mean of 50 could be the result of either of the following two sets of scores:

1. 48, 49, 50, 51, 52
2. 10, 20, 40, 80, 100

If we wanted to compare two such sets (one could represent scores on reading, while the other might be scores on listening), stating the mean alone would be misleading. We need an indication of the way that the scores are distributed around the mean. This is what the *standard deviation* gives us. The standard deviation for the two sets of the above sets of scores are 1) 1.58 and 2) 38.73.

The two summary measures, the mean and the standard deviation, thus allow us to compare the performance of different groups of students on a test, or the same group of students on different tests or different parts of one test. They will also prove useful in estimating the reliability of the test, below.

Box 2

Calculating means and standard deviations on a calculator

1. Press the key(s) necessary to engage the calculator's statistical functions.
2. Tap in the first score.
3. Press the *Enter* key (this is quite likely to have a plus (+) sign on it, though this varies from calculator to calculator).
4. Repeat 2 and 3 for all of the scores.
5. Press the *Mean* key, which probably has a X̄ sign on it.
    The figure which is then displayed is the mean of that set of scores.
6. Press the *Standard Deviation* key, which may have the Greek letter sigma (σ) on it. (If your calculator offers a choice of standard deviations – more than one key – use the one that the calculator manual says is based on a formula that contains the expression n–1, rather than just n.)
7. Record the mean and standard deviation, press the 'Clear' key, and then enter scores for the next component.

Histograms

The mean and standard deviation are numerical values. It is sometimes easier to 'take in' a set of scores pictorially as in the histogram, figure 1.

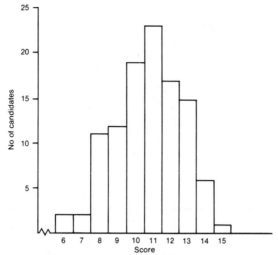

Figure 1. Histogram of Scores of 108 students on a 15 item test.

The diagram should be self-explanatory: the vertical dimension indicates the number of students scoring within a particular range of scores; the horizontal dimension shows what these ranges are.

Because of the ways a set of scores may be distributed (perhaps quite unevenly – for example a small number of very low scores, but no very high ones), such a pictorial representation can correct any misleading impression that the mean and standard deviation may give. It will also make clear what will be the outcome (how many will pass, fail, or be on the borderline) of setting particular pass marks. For these reasons, it is always advisable to make such a diagram, at least for test totals.

Estimating reliability

We already know from Chapter 5 that there are a number of ways of estimating a test's reliability. We shall present here only the *split half* method. It may be remembered that this involves dividing the test (or a component of a test) very carefully into two *equivalent* halves. Then for each student, two scores are calculated: the score on one part, and the score on the other part. The more similar are the two sets of scores, the more reliable is the test said to be (the rationale for this was presented in Chapter 5). Let us take the following sets of scores (for illustration only; estimates of reliability are only meaningful when the scores of much larger numbers of students are involved):

Appendix 1

TABLE I

Student	Score on one part	Score on other part
A	55	69
B	48	52
C	23	21
D	55	60
E	44	39
F	56	59
G	38	35
H	19	16
I	67	62
J	52	57

Box 3

Calculating the correlation coefficient on a calculator for the above split half scores

1. Press the key to engage the calculator's statistical functions.
2. Tap in 55.
3. Press one of the entry keys (the calculator manual will tell you which).
4. Tap in 69.
5. Press the other entry key.
6. Repeat 2 to 5 for the other pairs of scores.
7. Press the key for *Correlation coefficient* (probably marked 'r').

The strength of the relationship between the two sets of scores is given by the correlation coefficient. When calculated as directed in Box 3 above, this turns out to be 0.95. This coefficient relates to the two *half* tests. But the full test is of course twice as long as either half, and we know that the longer the test, other things being equal, the greater will be the reliability. So the full test should be more reliable than the coefficient of 0.95 would indicate. By means of a simple formula (the Spearman-Brown prophecy formula) it is possible to estimate the reliability of the whole test (see Box 4, below).

Box 4

Estimating reliability of full test from coefficient based on split halves

The formula to use is:

$$\text{Reliability of whole test} = \frac{2 \times \text{coefficient for split halves}}{1 + \text{coefficient for split halves}}$$

In the present case:
$$\frac{2 \times 0.95}{1 + 0.95}$$

$$= \frac{1.90}{1.95}$$

$$= 0.97$$

Using the formula, we obtain a figure of 0.97, which indicates very high reliability.

There is now just one thing to check. The possibility exists that the correlation coefficient has *overestimated* the level of agreement between the two sets of scores. For example, the following pairs of scores would give a perfect correlation coefficient of 1: 33, 66; 24, 48; 18, 36; 45, 90. Yet the two sets of scores are really very different. For this reason we should look at the means and standard deviations for the two halves (which can be obtained at the same time as the correlation coefficient, without putting in the scores all over again). These are: 45.7 and 15.2 for one part, 47.0 and 18.2 for the other.

The results for the two parts are sufficiently similar for us to believe that the correlation coefficient has not seriously overestimated the test's reliability.[2]

We are now in a position to calculate the *standard error of measurement.* (See Chapter 5 for a reminder of what this is and how it can be used.) Once more there is a simple formula, and its use is detailed in Box 5 below.

Box 5

Calculating the standard error of measurement

The formula is:

Standard error of measurement =
Stand Dev of test $\times \sqrt{1 - \text{reliability of test}}$

In the example we are using, the standard deviation of total test scores is 32.99 (combine part scores above if you want to check this).

So the standard error of measurement is
$$32.99 \times \sqrt{1 - 0.97}$$

$$= 32.99 \times \sqrt{0.03}$$

$$= 32.99 \times 0.173$$

$$= 5.7$$

---

2. The more correct methods for estimating reliability are based on what is called analysis of variance, which takes means and standard deviations into account from the outset. Analysis of variance is beyond the scope of this book, but see the *Further reading* section.

The standard error of measurement turns out to be 5.7. We know that we can be 95 per cent certain that an individual's true score will be within two standard errors of measurement from the score she or he actually obtains on the test. In this case, two standard errors of measurement amount to 11.4 (2 × 5.7). This means that for a candidate who scores 64 on the test we can be 95 per cent certain that the true score lies somewhere between 52.6 and 75.4. This is obviously valuable information if significant decisions are to be taken on the basis of such scores.

So far this Appendix has largely been concerned with obtaining useful information about the test as a whole. But a test is (normally) made up of parts, and it is useful to know how the various parts are contributing to the whole. If the test, or some part of it, is to be used again, it is essential to identify weaknesses. As a matter of course, the mean, standard deviation, and an estimate of reliability should be calculated for each part of the test. It is to be expected that the reliability of the parts will be lower than for the whole test, but if it is very low (significantly lower than most other parts) there would seem to be a need for revision; that part of the test is not contributing fully to the reliability of the whole.

It can also be revealing to look at the correlations between different parts with each other and with the total test.

Item analysis

Even individual items make their own contribution to the total test. Some contribute more than others, and it is the purpose of item analysis to identify those that need to be changed or replaced.

Item-test correlations

The assumption is made that, as a group, the people who do best on the whole test (or on some part of it being analysed) should do best on any particular item. The way that this is checked out is for the correlation to be calculated between total test scores (or total scores on a component, when different components are measuring distinct abilities) and scores on a particular item (zero for incorrect and 1 for correct, where scoring takes this form). Items that show correlations of 0.3 or more are generally considered satisfactory and to be contributing well to the total test. Items exhibiting lower correlations would seem not to be 'pulling their weight' and must be candidates for replacement or alteration. However, each such item has to be examined carefully and judged on its merits. There may be some good reason why performance on it (and possibly other similar items) does not fit well with total test performance. Items that correlate *negatively* with test totals (the calculator will show a negative sign) are highly suspect, since this indicates that the better you do on the test, the worse you will tend to do on this item.

Unless the tester has access to a computer, the calculation of item-test total correlations between scores on each item and scores on the whole test will be extremely tedious. Happily there are short cuts, one of which is represented in Figure 2 (an abac).

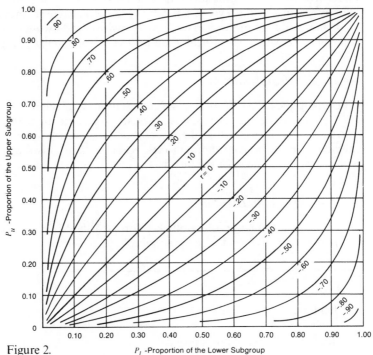

Figure 2. P_l -Proportion of the Lower Subgroup

(Downie and Heath 1965)

To use this, the 27 per cent of the students who do best on the test (the upper subgroup) have to be identified, as do the 27 per cent who do worst (the lower subgroup). Then for each item, one calculates the proportion of each subgroup who give the correct response. These two proportions are then used to enter the chart. If, for example, 75 per cent of the upper subgroup responded correctly on an item and 45 per cent of the lower subgroup did, then one would enter on the left-hand side at a point half-way between 0.70 and 0.80; and along the bottom at a point half-way between 0.40 and 0.50. Perpendicular lines drawn from these two points would meet just above the curved line marked '.30'. The estimate of the correlation between item scores and test scores is therefore just over 0.30. The item would seem to be performing satisfactorily.

Facility values

The proportion of students responding correctly to an item gives its facility value. Thus if 200 students take a test and 150 respond correctly to an item, that item's facility value is 0.75. There can be no strict rule about what range of facility values are to be regarded as satisfactory. It depends on what the purpose of the test is, and is related in a fairly complex fashion with item-test total correlations. The best advice that can be offered to the reader of this book is to consider the level of difficulty of the complete test. Should it be made more difficult or more easy? If so, knowledge of how individual items contribute to overall test difficulty can be used when making changes.

Analysis of distractors

Where multiple choice items are used, in addition to calculating item-test correlations and facility values, it is necessary to analyse the performance of distractors. Distractors which do not work, i.e. are chosen by very few candidates, make no contribution to test reliability. Such distractors have to be replaced by better ones, or the item has to be otherwise modified or dropped.

Item analysis record cards

Item analysis information is usefully kept on cards (either physically or in the computer). Here is an example for a multiple choice item.

Item No. ....

They'd said it would be a nice day, ... ?

a) wouldn't they?   b) didn't they?
c) hadn't they?   d) wouldn't it?   e) shouldn't it?

Option	Top 27%	Bottom 27%	Remainder
a	16	22	34
b	22	26	36
c	29	12	18
d	9	14	38
e	0	2	1
Nil	0	0	1

Facility value 0.21   *Item-test correlation 0.28*

From this it can be seen that though the item seems to be working well, the distractor e) is failing to distract candidates.

Item response theory

Everything that has been said so far has related to *classical* item analysis. In recent years new methods of analysis have been developed which have many attractions for the test writer. These all come under the general heading of item response theory, and the form of it so far most used in language testing is called 'Rasch analysis'. Unfortunately, for efficient use of this analysis quite powerful microcomputers are necessary. Nevertheless, the growing availability of these at reasonable cost means that the advantages of item response theory analysis will be possible for even small institutions. It will only be possible here to give the briefest outline of Rasch analysis.

Rasch analysis begins with the assumption that items on a test have a particular difficulty attached to them, that they can be placed in order of difficulty, and that the test taker has a fixed level of ability. Under these conditions, the idealised result of a number of candidates taking a test will be as in Table 2.

Table 2   Responses of imaginary subjects to imaginary items

Subjects	Items						
	1	2	3	4	5	6	7
1	1	0	0	0	0	0	0
2	1	1	1	0	0	0	0
3	1	1	1	0	0	0	0
4	1	1	1	0	0	0	0
5	1	1	1	1	0	0	0
6	1	1	1	1	1	0	0
7	1	1	1	1	1	0	0
8	1	1	1	1	1	1	1
Total incorrect	0	1	1	4	5	7	7

(Woods and Baker 1985)

Table 2 represents a model of what happens in test taking, but we know that, even if the model is correct, people's performance will not be a perfect reflection of their ability. In the real world we would expect an individual's performance more like:

   1 1 1 1 0 1 0 1 0

Rasch analysis in fact accepts variability of this kind as normal. But it does draw attention to test performance which is *significantly* different from what the model would predict. It will identify test takers whose behaviour does not fit the model; and it will identify *items* that do not fit the model. We know then that the total test scores of people so identified do not mean the same thing as (and so cannot be used in the same way as) the same score obtained by the other people taking the test. Similarly, the items which are identified as aberrant do not belong in the test; they should be modified (if it can be seen why they do not fit) or dropped.

There are a number of other features of Rasch analysis that makes it attractive to language testers. It seems likely that this form of analysis is going to become more popular, especially when its advantages are stressed and the rather forbidding mathematics that supports it is kept in the background. It has to be said, however, that Rasch analysis will not replace but will complement classical item analysis, and that the purpose of both is not to make decisions but to help testers to do so.

Further reading

For analysis of variance and statistical matters in general, see Woods, Fletcher, and Hughes (1986). For the calculation of reliability coefficients, see Krzanowski and Woods (1984). For item response theory, see Woods and Baker (1985) and other articles in *Language Testing* Vol. 2, No. 2. For statistical techniques for the analysis of criterion-referenced tests, see Hudson and Lynch (1984).

Appendix 2

Questions for the Oxford Examination in English as a foreign language New Zealand Youth Hostel passage (Chapter 11 Activities)

1. New Zealand has a) more than 60 hostels.
   b) less than 60 hostels.
   c) exactly 60 hostels.
2. You are unlikely to meet New Zealanders in the hostels.
   True or false? ....
3. Which hostel is said to be nearly always very full?..............................
4. Where can you visit a working sheep-station?...............................
5. Give one reason why Mount Cook is so popular with tourists.
   ....
6. What is the speciality of the hostel near the Franz Josef glacier?
   ....
7. Does the author recommend one particular hostel above any other which is particularly good for a lazy beach stay with sunbathing and scuba diving?
   ....
8. How many hostels cater for the Bay of Islands?...........
9. Name two cities which have two hostels.
   .... and ....
10. At which hostel can you definitely hire a bicycle? ....
11. You can wash your clothes in the hostels.
    True or false? ....
12. Why do Don and Jean Cameron think they will have to make a world trip next year?
    ....

Bibliography

Adams, M. L. and J. R. Frith (Eds.) 1979. *Testing Kit*. Washington D.C.: Foreign Service Institute.

Alderson, J. C. 1987. Innovation in language testing: Can the micro-computer help? *Language Testing Update Special Report No. 1*. Institute for English Language Education, University of Lancaster.

Alderson, J. C. and A. Hughes (Eds.) 1981. Issues in language testing. *ELT Documents 111*. London: The British Council.

Alderson, J. C., K. J. Krahnke, and C. W. Stansfield. 1987. *Reviews of English language proficiency tests*. Washington D.C.: TESOL.

Anastasi A. 1976. *Psychological testing* (4th edition). New York: Macmillan.

Bachman, L. F. and A. S. Palmer. 1981. The construct validation of the FSI oral interview. *Language Learning* 31:67–86.

Bachman, L. F. and A. S. Palmer. 1982. The construct validation of some components of communicative proficiency. *TESOL Quarterly* 16:449–65.

Bachman, L. F. and S. J. Savignon. 1986. The evaluation of communicative language proficiency: a critique of the ACTFL oral interview. *Modern Language Journal* 70:380–90.

Bozok, S. and A. Hughes. 1987. *Proceedings of the seminar, Testing English beyond the high school*. Istanbul: Boğaziçi University Publications.

Byrne, D. 1967 *Progressive picture compositions*. London: Longman.

Canale, M. and M. Swain, 1980. Theoretical bases of communicative approaches to second language teaching and testing. *Applied Linguistics* 1:1–47.

Carroll, J. B. 1961. Fundamental considerations in testing for English language proficiency of foreign students. In H. B. Allen and R. N. Campbell (Eds.) 1972. *Teaching English as a second language: a book of readings*. New York: McGraw Hill.

Carroll, J. B. 1981. Twenty-five years of research on foreign language aptitude. In K. C. Diller (Ed.) *Individual differences and universals in language learning aptitude*. Rowley, Mass: Newbury House.

Criper, C. and A. Davies. 1988. *ELTS validation project report*. Cambridge: The British Council and Cambridge Local Examinations Syndicate.

Crystal, D. and D. Davy. 1975. *Advanced conversational English*. London: Longman.

Davies, A. (Ed.) 1968. *Language testing symposium: a psycholinguistic perspective*. Oxford: Oxford University Press.

Davies, A. (1988). Communicative language testing. In Hughes 1988b.

Dexter, Colin. 1986. *The Secret of Annexe 3*. London. Macmillan.

Downie, N. M. and Robert W. Heath. 1985. *Basic Statistical Methods*. Harper and Row.

Ebel. R. L. 1978. The case for norm-referenced measurements. *Educational Researcher* 7 (11):3–5.

Garman, M. and A. Hughes 1983. *English cloze exercises*. Oxford: Blackwell.

Godshalk, F. I., F. Swineford, and W. E. Coffman 1966. *The measurement of writing ability*. New York: College Entrance Examination Board.

Greenberg, K. 1986. The development and validation of the TOEFL writing test: a discussion of TOEFL Research Reports 15 and 19. *TESOL Quarterly* 20:531–44.

Hamp-Lyons, E. 1987. Performance profiles for academic writing. In K. Bailey et al. (Eds.) 1987. *Language Testing Research: selected papers from the 1986 colloquium*. Monterey, California: Defense Language Institute.

Harris, D. P. 1968. *Testing English as a second language*. New York: McGraw Hill.

Hudson, T. and B. Lynch. 1984. A criterion-referenced approach to ESL achievement testing. *Language Testing* 1:171–201.

Hughes, A. 1981. Conversational cloze as a measure of oral ability. *English Language Teaching Journal* 35:161–8.

Hughes, A. 1986. A pragmatic approach to criterion-referenced foreign language testing. In Portal.

Hughes, A. 1988a. Introducing a needs-based test of English for study in an English medium university in Turkey. In Hughes 1988b.

Hughes, A. 1988b (Ed.) Testing English for university study. *ELT Documents 127*. Oxford: Modern English Press.

Hughes, A., L. Gülçur, P. Gürel, and T. McCombie. 1987. The new Boğaziçi University English Language Proficiency Test. In Bozok and Hughes.

Hughes, A. and D. Porter. (Eds.) 1983. *Current developments in language testing*. London: Academic Press.

Hughes, A., D. Porter, and C. Weir. (Eds.) 1988. *Validating the ELTS test: a critical review*. Cambridge: The British Council and University of Cambridge Local Examinations Syndicate.

Hughes, A. and P. Trudgill. 1987. *English accents and dialects: an introduction to social and regional varieties of British English* (2nd edition). London: Edward Arnold.

Jacobs, H. L., S. A. Zingraf, D. R. Wormuth, V. F. Hartfield, and J. B. Hughey. 1981. *Testing ESL composition: a practical approach*. Rowley, Mass: Newbury House.

Klein-Braley, C. 1985. A cloze-up on the C-Test: a study in the construct validation of authentic tests. *Language Testing* 2:76–104.

Klein-Braley, C. and U. Raatz. 1984. A survey of research on the C-Test. *Language Testing* 1:134–46.

Krzanowski, W. J. and A. J. Woods. 1984. Statistical aspects of reliability in language testing. *Language Testing* 1:1–20.

Lado, R. 1961. *Language testing*. London: Longman.

Lado, R. 1986. Analysis of native speaker performance on a cloze test. *Language Testing* 3:130–46.

Limb, S. 1983 Living with illness. Migraine. *The Observer*, 9 October.

Morrow, K. 1979. Communicative language testing: revolution or evolution? In C. J. Brumfit and K. Johnson. *The communicative approach to language teaching*. Oxford: Oxford University Press. Reprinted in Alderson and Hughes.

Morrow, K. 1986. The evaluation of tests of communicative performance. In Portal.

Oller, J. W. 1979. *Language tests at school: a pragmatic approach*. London: Longman.

Oller, J. W. (Ed.) 1983. *Issues in language testing research*. Rowley, Mass: Newbury House.

Oller, J. W. and C. A. Conrad. 1971. The cloze technique and ESL proficiency. *Language Learning* 21:183–94.

Pilliner, A. 1968. Subjective and objective testing. In Davies 1968.

Pimsleur P. 1968. Language aptitude testing. In Davies 1968.

Popham, W. J. 1978. The case for criterion-referenced measurements. *Educational Researcher* 7 (11):6–10.

Portal, M. (Ed.). 1986. *Innovations in language testing*. Windsor: NFER-Nelson.

Shohamy, E. 1984. Does the testing method make a difference? The case of reading comprehension. *Language Testing* 1:147–76.

Shohamy, E., T. Reves, and Y. Bejarano. 1986. Introducing a new comprehensive test of oral proficiency. *English Language Teaching Journal* 40: 212–20.

Skehan, P. 1984. Issues in the testing of English for specific purposes. *Language Testing* 1: 202–20.

Skehan, P. 1986. The role of foreign language aptitude in a model of school learning. *Language Testing* 3:188–221.

Spolsky, B. 1981. Some ethical questions about language testing. In C. Klein-Braley and D. K. Stevenson (Eds.) *Practice and problems in language testing 1*. Frankfurt: Verlag Peter D. Lang.

Streiff, V. 1978. Relations among oral and written cloze scores and achievement test scores in a bilingual setting. In J. W. Oller and K. Perkins (Eds.) *Language in education: testing the tests*. Rowley, Mass: Newbury House.

Swan, M. 1975. *Inside meaning*. Cambridge: Cambridge University Press.

Swan, M. and C. Walter. 1988. *The Cambridge English Course. Student's Book 3*. Cambridge: Cambridge University Press.

Timmins, N. 1987. Passive smoking comes under official fire. *The Independent*, 14 March.

Trudgill, P. and J. Hannah. 1982. *International English: a guide to the varieties of standard English*. London: Edward Arnold.

Underhill, N. 1987. *Testing spoken language: a handbook of oral testing techniques*. Cambridge: Cambridge University Press.

Weir, C. J. 1988a. *Communicative language testing*. Exeter Linguistic Studies, Vol 11. Exeter: University of Exeter.

Weir, C. J. 1988b. The specification, realization and validation of an English language proficiency test. In Hughes, 1988b.

West, M. (Ed.) 1953. *A general service list of English words: with semantic frequencies and a supplementary word-list for the writing of popular science and technology*. London: Longman.

Woods, A., and R. Baker. 1985. Item response theory. *Language Testing* 2:119–40.

Woods, A., P. Fletcher, and A. Hughes. 1986. *Statistics in language studies.* Cambridge: Cambridge University Press.

Index